Managing Workp

Managing Workplace Stress

A Best Practice Blueprint

STEPHEN WILLIAMS
LESLEY COOPER

JOHN WILEY & SONS, LTD

Other Wiley Editorial Offices

John Wiley & Sons, Inc., 605 Third Avenue,
New York, NY 10158-0012, USA

WILEY-VCH Verlag GmbH, Pappelallee 3,
D-69469 Weinheim, Germany

John Wiley & Sons Australia Ltd, 33 Park Road, Milton,
Queensland 4064, Australia

John Wiley & Sons (Asia) Pte Ltd, 2 Clementi Loop #02-01,
Jin Xing Distripark, Singapore 129809

John Wiley & Sons (Canada) Ltd, 22 Worcester Road,
Rexdale, Ontario M9W 1L1, Canada

British Library Cataloguing in Publication Data

A catalogue record for this book is available from the British Library

ISBN 0-470-84287-3

Typeset in 11/15.5pt ITC Garamond Light by Footnote Graphics, Warminster, Wiltshire.
Printed and bound in Great Britain by Biddles Ltd, Guildford and King's Lynn.
This book is printed on acid-free paper responsibly manufactured from sustainable forestry, in
which at least two trees are planted for each one used for paper production.

Contents

Series Foreword

I am delighted to be able to introduce to you the *CBI Fast Track Series*. The book you are holding is the outcome of a significant new publishing partnership between the CBI and John Wiley & Sons (Wiley). We intend it to be the first in a long line of high quality materials on which the CBI and Wiley collaborate. Before saying a little about this partnership, I would like to briefly introduce you to the CBI.

With a direct corporate membership employing over 4 million and a trade association membership representing over 6 million of the workforce, the CBI is the premier organisation speaking for companies in the UK. We represent directly and indirectly, over 200 000 companies employing more than 40% of the UK private sector workforce. The majority of blue-chip organisations and industry leaders from the FTSE 250 are members, as well as a significant number of small to medium sized companies (SMEs).* Our mission is to ensure that the government of the day, Whitehall, Brussels and the wider community understand the needs of British business. The CBI takes an active role in forming policies that enable UK companies to compete and prosper, and we ensure that the lines of communication between private and public leaders are always open on a national scale as well as via our regional networks.

The appropriateness of a link between the CBI and a leading business publisher like Wiley cannot be understated. Both organisations have a vested interest in efficiently and effectively serving the needs of businesses of all sizes. Both are forward-thinkers; constantly trend-spotting to envision where the next issues and concerns lie. Both maintain a global outlook in servicing the needs of its local customers. And finally, both champion the adoption of best practice amongst the groups they represent.

Which brings us back to this series. Each *CBI Fast Track* book offers a complete best practice briefing in a selected topic, along with a blueprint for successful implementation. The aim is to help enterprises achieve peak performance across key disciplines. The series will continue to evolve as new and different issues force their way to the top of the corporate agenda.

I do hope you enjoy this book and would encourage you to look out for further titles from the CBI and Wiley. Here's to all the opportunities the future holds and to *Fast Track* success with your own corporate agenda.

*Foreign companies that maintain registered offices in the UK are also eligible for CBI membership.

Digby Jones
Director-General, CBI

THE VOICE OF BUSINESS

About the authors

Stephen Williams

Dr Stephen Williams is the founder of Resource Systems, a human resource consultancy specialising in improving workplace wellbeing, managing the consequences of organisational change, and helping organisations to increase the effectiveness of their recruitment and retention practices.

Stephen is an organisational psychologist with a background in HR management. His contribution to the management of employee wellbeing has been recognised with his election as an Honorary Fellow of the Faculty of Occupational Medicine. He is also an Honorary Member of the Society of Occupational Medicine. His consultancy work includes advising major organisations in the UK and US on the measurement and management of employee wellbeing and the development of appropriate interventions.

Stephen's PhD research led to the development of the Pressure Management Indicator (PMI), a highly effective stress management questionnaire and profiling tool available in seven languages and used extensively throughout the world in the areas of pressure management, organisational development, training, and occupational health.

Stephen is a frequent speaker at international conferences on occupational stress, releasing individual potential, employee wellbeing, and other management issues.

Lesley Cooper

Lesley Cooper is the founder of WorkingWell Limited, a specialist health management consultancy whose focus is the proactive and cost effective management of employee wellbeing. A health management consultant with a broad business background, she has a detailed knowledge of the practical considerations surrounding the delivery of occupational health care and the management of employee health risks.

Her business background, gained in both managerial and operational environments, gives her sharp insight into the commercial imperatives behind investment in employee health and wellbeing, as well as the costs of failure to manage workplace wellbeing effectively. Lesley has particular interest and expertise in the measurement and management of occupational stress and has considerable experience in the delivery of both large- and small-scale stress audit programmes gained through working closely with major UK companies.

She is a regular speaker at international events on the subjects of occupational stress, employee wellbeing and the relationship between employee health and business success. She has also contributed to a number of TV and Radio programmes on the subject of employee wellbeing, most recently, along with Dr Stephen Williams, Channel 4's highly acclaimed documentary 'Stressed Out'.

Stephen Williams and Lesley Cooper are two of the country's leading experts in the applied management of workplace stress. The principles outlined in this best practice guide have been developed through their experience of conducting hundreds of stress audits in a wide variety of public and private sector organisations in the UK and overseas.

Stephen and Lesley are the co-authors of *Dangerous Waters: Strategies for Improving Wellbeing at Work* (April 1999), published by John Wiley & Sons.

Introduction

Stress is a fact of modern-day life. It is all around us and, sooner or later, it will almost certainly affect everyone. It affects people directly when they themselves are under stress and it affects them indirectly when the people they work with or the people they live with suffer from stress. Stress damages people at home, at work, and in the difficult boundary between home and work. Even the most conservative estimates of the damage caused to people by stress make it a significant issue for individual health and economic prosperity. The impact of workplace stress should not be under-estimated. It is seen in the human cost of ill health, broken relation-ships, career failure, and wasted lives. It is also present in the commercial costs of lower productivity, reduced performance, poor customer service and failure of innovation.

Academic experts and media stress gurus may not be able to agree on a detailed definition of stress but they know that stress is out there – and that it's bad for people! Almost every week the news-papers, television and radio carry another story about the 'epidemic' of stress at work. The stories are either sensational headlines about huge pay-outs for stress-related ill health or the horrors of stress-inducing bosses, stress-related illness and family break-up or, at its most extreme, work-related suicide. With this background of media attention and a lack of clarity and consistency from the 'stress professionals' it's not surprising that managers and their staff are confused!

Our purpose in writing this book is to explain why stress is an important issue for everyone at work and provide a structured approach – a clear blueprint for the effective management of work-place stress. The approach is simple and straightforward: collect the evidence, understand the issues, interpret the information and take appropriate action. Although we will explain what stress is and what it does we will not dwell on definitions or theoretical models. To provide a clear blueprint we need to deal with the real issues of workplace stress, not the myths.

Too many options – so many roads

Sooner or later almost every manager will have to deal with the problem of stress at work. The owner manager of a small business may want to understand why her staff are continually taking days off for no obvious reason. The middle manager in a medium size firm wants to know why his staff are uncooperative, rude to customers and each other and never seem to do anything unless they're forced. The chief executive of a large multinational wants to find out why creativity and innovation are being stifled. There is no escape from either the direct threat of a claim for stress-related illness or the damaging consequences of a disaffected and disillusioned work-force.

Unfortunately, no clear solutions are immediately apparent. Managers looking for outside help will find a bewildering array of choices. The stress industry is big business – there are counsellors, psychotherapists, stress consultants, trainers, health and fitness experts, aromatherapists and any number of other experts eager to get on the stress bandwagon. Within the organisation it's difficult to know where to go for help. Is stress the responsibility of line managers? Do HR (the human resources department) have relevant expertise? If you are fortunate enough to have a company occupational health service then they should be able to provide expert advice but their knowledge of best practice may be out of date or anchored in an inappropriate medical model that only sees stress as an individual's illness and not as a sign of managerial malaise. There are so many choices, so many roads to follow with little assurance that any of them will lead to a successful resolution of your specific concerns.

And that's the point – stress is so hard to define and so difficult to manage precisely because it is so variable. It's hard to know what to do because stress takes so many forms. For one person stress can manifest itself as a deep tearful depression characterised by lethargy and exhaustion, for someone else it can be seen as manic obsessive behaviours, working all hours with a sense of increasing desperation. One of these people's stress may be caused by too much to do and not enough time to do it in; the other person's stress could be a result of too little work with too much time doing nothing and insufficient challenge. To make matters even more complicated; both these people could be doing the same job in the same department – yours!

A clear path

This book is intended to cut through the confusion, to provide a practical systematic approach to managing stress at work – in whatever form it occurs. The overall message is very simple – diagnose before treatment! Find out what is going on and take appropriate action.

We believe that the systematic method outlined in this book will be of benefit to people in organisations who want to understand the issues before providing the remedies. We firmly believe that diagnosis should precede treatment and that it is better to act on fact rather than anecdote. Many of the 'facts' and evidence that you need are all around you, if you know where to look. This book is written to help you find out what you need to know, using the resources and information that you already have or can find from within your organisation. It is also designed to help you identify for yourself when you may need to call on expert help and supplement your knowledge using external resources.

Managing stress begins with the recognition that people, however superficially robust, are vulnerable. No one, not even the most resilient manager or employee, can work under excessive pressure forever. We all have a point at which we break. We need to get below the surface gloss of apparent coping and try to understand what is really going on inside our people. How do we know if someone is coping well or if they are just covering up an impending disaster?

How can a line manager tell who's about to fall off the edge because of excessive demands or who's frustrated because they are insufficiently challenged, and are any of the staff really coping with what's going on? These are the fundamental questions that need to be addressed if we are to create a working environment in which we have identified and, wherever possible, eliminated the risks of stress-related illness.

ONE

What is Stress?

Stress damages people and it damages their organisations. It can be all-pervasive. It can affect people in all occupations and of all ages irrespective of sex, nationality, educational background or role. Work-related stress is estimated to affect at least a third of the workforce in any one year. It costs organisations billions of pounds a year in lost productivity and accounts for over half the working days lost through sickness absence. Stress has been linked to a wide variety of diseases and the European Foundation estimates that lifestyle and stress-related illness accounts for at least half of all premature deaths. Although the 'official' figures for the cost of stress vary widely, they have one common feature – they are all massive. They reflect, however imprecisely, a huge cost to individuals and to organisations. The cost isn't just financial; there is a mental, physical and social cost as well. The evidence for stress-related ill health is all around us. Look within your organisation. If you are typical of other UK businesses, it's likely that 10% of your workforce report very low levels of satisfaction with both their jobs and the organisation. Twenty per cent of your staff will report they have suffered some major life event in the past three months and approximately 3% will report levels of mental ill health that are worse than those of psychiatric outpatients receiving clinical treatment for anxiety and depression.

When it comes to something as potentially damaging and disruptive as workplace stress, the human and commercial costs are too vast to be approached from a position of anecdote and intuition. Occupational stress needs to be addressed in a structured and effective manner as part of an overall strategy for improving well-being at work.

Managers in most organisations recognise that there is some stress amongst their workforce. They may be able to tell you where they think it comes from and may even be able to articulate how they see the issue affecting their efficiency, productivity and competitive advantage. However, being aware of the existence of the problem is not enough to be able to start the process of managing it. Stress is a complex issue. The interplay of a wide range of factors from home, from work and the interface between home and work makes it difficult to separate cause from effect and, in the vast majority of cases, almost impossible to pinpoint one event or incident that 'caused' the stress problem. The variability of the stress process means that managers and researchers are trying to hit a moving target. For the individual, stress may manifest itself as a headache one day, an upset stomach or a sleepless night the next. For the manager, one of her staff may show they are suffering stress by becoming argumentative and abrasive, another may become withdrawn and timid.

It is this wide variety of symptoms and causes and the complex interrelationship between factors that makes stress at work so difficult to manage. Each of the outcomes of the stress process may have multiple causes, only a few of which may be related to workplace issues. Different people will react to the same event in many different ways with different outcomes, some of which may be beneficial whilst others are extremely damaging. It is not surprising that many organisations shy away from trying to make sense of this complex mixture of misunderstood variables and rely on counselling or stress management training to 'deal with stress'. Unfortunately, as we will discuss in more detail later, treatment on its own isn't enough. Counselling and stress management courses may help some individuals to manage their symptoms but they rarely address the factors that caused their stress and these will continue to damage the individual and the organisation. It's like taking fish out of a polluted pool, cleaning them up, and then throwing them back in. The fish will continue to suffer until the water is cleaned up. However, to ensure that the fish stay healthy, cleaning the water is not enough. The pollution has to be stopped at source. That involves finding the source and taking appropriate action. It's the same with people and their organisations; to achieve lasting benefit you have to find out what's causing workplace stress and stop it at its source. It is vitally important to treat the casualties but this must be done in the context of addressing the factors that caused them to become casualties in the first place.

Sending people for counselling who are ill or running a few stress management workshops is simple and straightforward. It doesn't threaten working practices, doesn't take too much time and doesn't raise issues that many managers would rather ignore. Unfortunately it doesn't provide a lasting solution. The answer is to identify and manage the causes of stress as well as its effects by adopting a systematic, structured approach that recognises the difficulties of addressing the root causes and offers a simple, clear process based on small steps for sustainable change.

The process starts with identifying what we know. It's very difficult, if not impossible, to completely understand all of the issues so we should accept that our knowledge of the process does not have to be perfect in order for us to make a difference. There are parallels with a wide range of physiological and medical interventions. For example, we know that there are many common risk factors – such as: smoking, drinking, diet, exercise, and hereditary factors – that contribute toward coronary heart disease but we can still only explain a small proportion of the variance in the onset of the disease. We recognise that many of the risk factors are interrelated and that each unique combination may have a different impact on the onset of illness. This is also the case with occupational stress. We can identify a variety of issues that are known to influence levels of stress and we know that these occur in different combinations for each individual. We do not know enough to be able to predict that one particular person, when exposed to these pressures, will develop a specific set of illnesses but we can say that a proportion of the people will be affected. We can go on to demonstrate that, if we remove some of these pressures, people will, on the whole, improve. The science may not be precise but it's good enough to make things better. In the real world if we have good evidence of the relationship between the causes and the outcomes and can show that removing a source of pressure leads to an improvement in wellbeing then, we don't necessarily need to know precisely how it works. In the practical, pragmatic management of workplace stress, close can be good enough.

The need to understand

In order to effectively manage the stress process we need to act on facts, not anecdote. We need to collect the evidence that will enable us to identify the key issues. We need to improve our level of understanding and we need a framework in which to operate. This requires a good working model of the stress process that can be empirically tested and used to design interventions that produce sustainable and observable improvement. The first priority for this model is that it helps people to understand that stress can be managed and that this complicated, multifaceted problem can be reduced to simpler, more manageable components.

The first task is therefore to break through the ignorance barrier and help people, both managers and staff, to realise that stress at work can be managed. It doesn't have to be endured. Stress may be endemic but it isn't inevitable.

Stress Defined

One of the first steps in an effective strategy for managing stress is to reach a common understanding of what is meant by the term 'stress'. To cut through the confusion we need a useable working definition and a clear understanding of the words we use to talk about stress. One of the easiest initiatives an organisation can take in starting to manage stress at work is to adopt a common language for talking about it. We have found that something as simple as separating pressure – the demands or challenges facing people – from stress – the unwanted outcome of too much pressure – makes a big difference to the way people approach the problem. Focusing attention on how to reduce or remove specific sources of pressure is much easier than trying to come to grips with something as vague and as emotive as the word 'stress'.

The stress model

Experts talk about stress in a variety of ways: they mention stressors, pressures, demands, and they talk about good and bad stress, eustress (bad stress as opposed to good stress) and distress. As almost every book on stress defines the term in a different way it's not surprising that people find it hard to recognise and manage workplace stress. In order to raise awareness and help people in your organisation to manage stress you need a clear definition and a simple model that makes sense and can act as a framework on which to build appropriate interventions. Our model starts with the *dynamics* of the stress process and describes it in terms of inputs, outcomes and individual differences. The model is like a simple manufacturing process, say for making pottery.

The process starts with the raw materials, the inputs. In making pottery this is the clay and the water. However, each of the raw materials, the different types of clay that are used to make the pots, are not identical; they have different sizes, different qualities, and will react differently to the process. The differences in the raw materials influence the quality of the end-product. In the case of stress these differences are people's personalities and behaviours, the factors that make each of us a unique individual. The clay is fired in a kiln where the raw material is exposed to high temperatures for a long period; in our analogy, these are the pressures, the demands we place on people. When we take out the finished product we can see the outcome of the process. When we look at the finished pottery, we notice that not all the pots are the same. Although all of the raw material has been through the same process, baked at the same temperature for the same time, some pieces have become strong and kept their shape, others have cracked, distorted, or crumbled. It's like this with people – only more complicated! We put our people under pressure and expect them to react in the same way. They don't! Some thrive, some survive and some break.

To manage stress effectively we need to know why and how this happens. We also need to realise that sometimes we get it completely wrong. We raise the temperature too high, leave the clay in for too long, or miss out an essential ingredient. Then we ruin the entire batch. Sometimes we put our people under just too much pressure or we keep the pressure up for just too long and, in different ways, they all suffer. To understand why this happens and to increase the probability that we get healthy outcomes we need to understand the process and quantify the variables.

Stress therefore is an outcome. It is the end of the process, not the beginning. The start of the process, the raw material, is the people. We are all different; to quote Ralph Waldo Emerson, 'We boil at different degrees.' Life, at work and at home, puts people under pressure. Pressure is felt as the range of problems, demands or challenges that we encounter at work and in the rest of our lives.

The 4-way model of stress

Just as there are many different definitions of stress there are many different models of the stress process. In explaining the factors that need to be measured in analysing stress at work we use a simple, mechanistic model to describe the various elements of the stress process and show how these elements are interrelated. We call this the four-way model of stress (see Figure 1.1).

The model illustrates the dynamics of the stress process. It shows the sources of pressure, and how they are moderated or amplified by personality and behavioural characteristics. It also shows the counterbalancing effect of coping and support. The end box is the effect of the interaction between pressures, individual characteristics and coping in terms of positive and negative health and wellbeing outcomes. The way that the pointer moves up and down depends on the relative strength of those factors for an individual.

The better and more varied our coping mechanisms, the larger the counterbalancing force pushing the pointer toward the positive end of the scale. Good coping generates an additional benefit; as the better we cope, the more we feel in control and the higher our self-

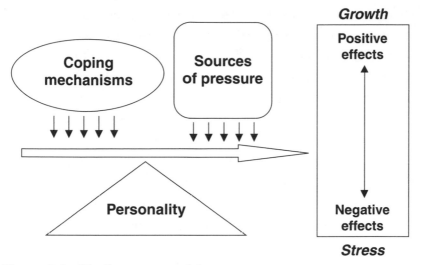

Figure 1.1   *The Four-way model*

esteem. This, in turn, produces a positive feedback loop in which better coping leads to raised self-esteem, which is itself another coping skill – a virtuous circle of effective pressure management.

People experience an increase in self-confidence and self-esteem when they succeed in managing pressure (The more we do, the more we're capable of doing) When someone feels they are doing a good job, that they're valued and appreciated, they become more confident of themselves and better able to cope. Instead of the vicious circle that occurs when people can't cope we have a virtuous circle of positive self-reinforcement.

Stress is a personal response and is the negative outcome of an imbalance between pressure and the person's ability to cope with that pressure. Stress is the way I feel when it's all too much; it's the knot in the stomach, the tension in the shoulders, the inability to sleep, the problems with behaviour, and so forth. These are the physical, mental and social signs that we can no longer cope.

If we separate the factors involved in the stress process in this way then we have a model for understanding that is straightforward and makes sense to most people.

It is the differences between each of us as individuals that make managing stress so challenging. When we understand why similar levels of pressure affect different people in different ways we can start to manage pressure at the individual rather than the group level. We can take steps to make sure we know how our people will react to different pressures, who is likely to thrive and who will fall apart, and we can change the nature or the extent of the pressure for each individual to get the most out of each of them without damage. As this book will make clear, proactive stress management places more emphasis on preventing stress than on treating the symptoms. We recognise that both prevention and treatment are important and we know that treatment on its own is not enough. Pressure must be addressed at source; otherwise the same problems will keep reoccurring, and time, effort and resources will be wasted on a perpetual round of 'patching up' the casualties. The prevention process begins with understanding the specific issues that affect your workforce. Every workplace is different and there is no universal source of pressure and no standard outcome from it.

Individual differences

We interpret events in different ways, have different personalities and ways of behaving that moderate or exacerbate the pressures of life. We all have different ways of coping and varying amounts of support available to us either practically or socially. The stress model is dynamic; it reflects the changeable interrelationship that exists between perceived pressure, individual personality differences and personal coping skills. When the level of pressure is within the individual's capacity to cope then the outcomes are positive and can result in personal growth. We need some pressure to stimulate personal growth and development – but we don't need too much! (see Figure 1.2). Growth occurs when the individual is able to adapt to or overcome the challenges or pressures in their life.

When the pressures on us exceed our capacity to cope then the outcome is not growth but something far less positive – stress (see Figure 1.3).

A further definition of stress is as a negative effect that occurs when the perceived pressure on an individual exceeds their perceived ability to cope. The reason perception is in the definition

Figure 1.2 *Pressure leads to growth*

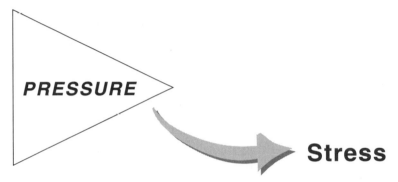

Figure 1.3 *Pressure leads to stress*

twice is because it's not about reality. It's not about whether I've *actually* got too many demands upon me or whether life is hard or whatever. It's about what I think it is and it's also whether I feel I can cope or not. The simpler version of this definition is that 'stress is what you feel when you just can't cope'.

This definition implies a sense of hopelessness or despair; it's a recognition that life is out of balance, that it's all too much. It may be a temporary imbalance lasting just a few hours or it could be a longer-term chronic condition. It is about self-perception and your own feelings, and therefore it requires you to be aware of how you feel. Unfortunately, one of the effects of stress is that we lose the capacity for self-awareness; we are too busy or too out of control to stop and notice how badly we are coping. It's only later, either when we've come through the experience and look back or, for some less fortunate people, when we collapse, that we realise how stressed we were. We need to be aware of a general sense of discomfort, that something isn't quite right and check to see if we really are coping and, if not, what do we need to do to get back in control. The sooner we are aware of stress the quicker we can start to take action and the easier it is to make changes.

Understanding more about the individual stress response is therefore about increasing your awareness of where you are on each of the different aspects of the model in Figure 1.1. Where are the pressures coming from? What is it about me that helps me to feel I can cope with those things or not? What are the outcomes for me in terms of stress or growth?

The 4-way model implies that stress is not an inevitable outcome of pressure. We can be under pressure and not suffer from stress. The pressures or demands placed upon us can also produce positive outcomes that lead to personal growth.

For example, how many people, when they first learnt to drive, got into the car, felt calm and relaxed, laid back in the seat, put the stereo on, revved the engine and just zoomed off, chatting to the passengers? It doesn't happen like that. Most people have a different experience; they may be tense or apprehensive, perhaps anxious about what's going to happen. They sit upright, shoulders stiff, staring ahead, hands clenched on the wheel. But at the end of the lesson, providing that they got through the ordeal without too many incidents, there's a feeling of release and relaxation. As the tension disappears they feel good, and the second lesson is just that bit easier. With practice the stress disappears altogether, at least until the day of the driving test! What has happened is that the learner driver has been under pressure, has felt threatened – psychologically if not physically – and has overcome that challenge and grown as a result. The outcome was positive, not negative. It produced growth, not stress.

The stress response

So, now we've defined stress, we need to know what it does to us and how we can recognise it. Why does being under pressure from too much or too little work, poor relationships at work, or feeling that we have little influence on the way we work, have such a profound effect on our bodies? Surely, it's all in the mind?

To understand this we need to look back over human evolution. What got us here? What factors helped us to survive into the twenty-first century in the face of ever-present, life-threatening physical danger? The answer lies in the fight or flight response, the massive changes in our physiology and body chemistry triggered in response to danger that could make all the difference between life and death.

In the fight or flight response a whole range of chemicals and hormones are released into our bodies to mobilise our resources in order to maximise the probability of short-term survival. This produces a wide range of effects including:

- Increased heart rate
- Increased respiration rate
- Increased blood supply to brain
- Dilated pupils
- Dry mouth
- Sweating
- Reduction in blood supply to less vital organs.

To some extent these responses can still be useful in our modern age, as anyone who has stepped from a kerb into the path of an oncoming truck will tell you (if they got back on the kerb in time, that is!). The problem is that most of the threats we face now are more likely to be psychological than physical. Unfortunately, we only have one response! Once we become aware of a possible threat, whether real or imagined, we respond as if the threat were physical. The heart rate increases to speed up delivery of blood to the muscles, pupils dilate to increase the amount of light into the eye and selected blood vessels contract to divert blood away from the less vital organs into the muscles that will help us fight or run away.

These physical changes developed to provide a temporary short-term boost. Once the threat has passed our nervous system triggers another set of chemical and hormonal changes to return our physiology and biochemistry to normal functioning. In the past this system worked well. A short-term disruption was followed by a return to normality.

Unfortunately modern life isn't so simple. Threats are no longer isolated events. When the threats that trigger the fight or flight response are repeated or prolonged and our bodies continue to react, then our ability to adapt eventually becomes exhausted and we start to suffer from stress.

Instead of the short-term effects – such as a temporary increase in heart rate, change in muscle tension, sweating and so on – there will be physical and emotional signs to signal that pressure has turned into stress. The following list shows some of the more common physical and behavioural symptoms of the stress process:

Physical
- Altered sleep patterns, e.g., difficulty getting to sleep, early waking
- Tiredness
- Lethargy
- Breathlessness, bouts of dizziness, light-headedness
- Indigestion, heartburn
- Nausea
- Bowel disturbance, e.g., diarrhoea, constipation
- Headaches
- Loss of sexual drive
- Muscle tension, e.g., neck pain, back pain
- Nervous twitches

Behavioural
- Irritability and aggression
- Anxiety and apprehension
- Poor decision-making
- Preoccupation with trivia
- Inability to prioritise
- Difficulty in coping
- Mood changes and swings
- Difficulty in concentrating

- Deterioration in recent memory
- Feelings of failure
- Lack of self-worth
- Isolation.

Different people produce different symptoms under stress and it helps to learn to recognise the body's response. Stress is a complex subject and the precise relationship between stress and physical illnesses is not clearly understood. It is, however, recognised as a contributory factor in many illnesses.

Faced with a threatening or disturbing situation with a client or colleague, geared up for flight (or fight) in the boardroom, call centre, workshop or sales floor – we have nowhere to go. Neither fight nor flight in these circumstances is likely to be desirable or lead to continued employment. But these are now the situations in which we find ourselves exposed to a threat most often, and, as a result, the evolutionary response is no longer appropriate. The key point to remember about the stress response is that it is a built-in survival mechanism. It is part of our evolutionary heritage and we shouldn't be ashamed or embarrassed about feeling stressed. In the words of Dr Noel McElearney, Medical Director, Scottish & Newcastle plc: 'Stress isn't about being weak, it's about being human.'

The long-term effects

The effect on the body of long-term exposure to stressful situations is becoming better understood and there is growing acceptance that a good deal of physical ill health may be attributed to long-term exposure to stress. The biochemical changes in the body that are triggered as a short-term survival mechanism have the complete opposite effect if their presence is prolonged. Far from performing a protective function, these factors can seriously undermine the body's ability to protect itself. Constant readiness for 'fight or flight' means that adrenaline is constantly present in the bloodstream. One of the many results of this constant 'adrenalisation' is to depress the immune system, with the corresponding result that the person has reduced resistance to coughs and colds and other infectious complaints. Thus a general level of ill health, frequent infections and general debility are some of the more easily observable long-term effects.

Of even greater concern though is the mounting evidence that stress is likely to be a causal factor in more life-threatening conditions. In 'Jobs don't kill people, but stress in the workplace can' the *Boston Globe* reported on what they described as one of the most comprehensive US studies so far of hypertension and job strain. In this study researchers saw a clear link between job strain – defined as being in a job with high demands but low control over working conditions – and higher rates of heart disease and other physical ailments. In a study of nearly 200 men over a three-year period there was a clear correlation between those with the most job strain and significantly higher blood pressure.

Around the world, scientists have been looking at the influence of job strain on heart disease, immune system function, gastrointestinal illness, back and joint pain and depression. Some very clear relationships are starting to emerge. Many of the life-threatening complaints that employees develop may therefore be a consequence, either direct or indirect, of long-term stress.

TWO

How to Recognise
Workplace Stress

We said in Chapter 1 that the evidence you need to make your own assessment of stress at work is all around you, if you know where to look. Part of the process of becoming better able to read the signs of organisational stress more clearly is being able to recognise stress in yourself and others. But what are the signs, for individual employees and for groups of employees? What is it, as you look around your organisation, that will help you to evaluate the extent to which stress is or is not an issue for your staff?

We have seen that our bodies respond to a perceived threat by releasing a range of chemicals and hormones that change our blood chemistry and physiology. Improving our ability to observe the signs and symptoms starts with thinking about the kind of questions that people ask themselves when things start to go wrong at work. Why do I take on more work? Why do I get tense? Why don't I get to finish anything? Why do I get so many colds? Why am I always irritable? (see Figure 2.1).

Figure 2.1 *It's hard to understand – individuals*

You can look at some individuals and see that it's obvious that there's a problem. There may be far too much work coming in and not enough going out so that they are still at work at seven at night or they come in at six in the morning. The workload never decreases and the employee, exhausted mentally and physically, hovers on the brink of collapse.

One of the problems in trying to identify the level of stress in an organisation is that exactly the same doubts and fears are expressed by people who, to the outside world, look absolutely fine. They look as if they're coping with pressure and will not complain about their workload, their hours or their boss. They may sit at their desk tense with frustration or anger, they may vent their feelings on the family or their friends but they won't say a word to their managers! The problem is further compounded by the fact that many individuals who are actually suffering the symptoms of stress may not actually be aware that they are having difficulty coping. They may recognise that they are feeling under pressure all of the time, are irritable, have difficulty concentrating and lack energy or confidence, but they do not equate these symptoms with an imbalance between the pressure they are under and their ability to cope with that pressure. If they are fortunate their family, friends, manager or colleagues may see the signs and help them to recognise that things are getting out of control. But far too many people continue in almost complete ignorance of their deteriorating condition until they collapse, break down or suffer serious ill health. The warning signs are there – but we don't see them or don't understand what they mean until it is too late.

Signs of stress

Signs are the outward manifestation of stress. We listed some of the symptoms of stress in the previous chapter, but how do we see those symptoms manifested in others? Usually the strongest indicator that something is wrong is a change in the way people behave. This could be a change in appearance, in behaviour, or in habits. The following list describes some of the changes that may indicate that someone is suffering from stress:

Altered appearance

- lack of care in appearance
- looks miserable
- looks tired
- looks nervous, apprehensive
- looks agitated

Altered habits

- eating more, eating less
- drinking more
- smoking more
- increased absence
- more accident prone

Altered behaviour

- irritability
- aggression
- mood swings
- poor concentration
- poor decision-making
- reduced performance.

The above isn't a complete list of all the signs of stress and, of course, many of these signs may be unconnected with stress; some of the changes in appearance, for example, could simply indicate the after-effects of a very good night out!

Understanding the impact on the organisation

At the start of this chapter we said how difficult it was with some employees to see signs and symptoms that stress exists. Individuals manifest the effects in different ways, with some effects being more observable than others. In the same way that individuals start to become aware of stress as an underlying cause of their ill health or impaired wellbeing with questions to themselves like 'Why don't I get to finish anything?' or 'Why do I get so many colds?'; managers can ask themselves similar questions about their staff. Why do people make so many mistakes around here? What happened to creativity and innovation? Why is the business doing badly? Why is productivity falling? Why are so many people absent? Why is staff turnover rising? Why do we seem to be making so many mistakes? (see Figure 2.2).

Managers can and often do puzzle over the answers to these questions. Much less frequently they arrive at the conclusion that workplace stress is likely to be the major contributor. This is a dangerous oversight. Increased staff turnover, sickness absence, lower productivity and higher accident and error rates are all clear indicators of workplace stress.

These organisational signs that all is not well are relatively easy to see. In practical terms they are often easier to observe than signs of stress in the individual. Organisations are generally very good at monitoring their performance and there are relatively few areas of commercial activity that are not regularly measured and reported. Unfortunately, companies usually know considerably less about the people who work for them and even relatively visible warning signs are often ignored. Some managers miss the signs because they're just too busy looking the other way. Others manage their people to

Figure 2.2 *It's hard to understand – managers*

the best of their ability but they are too busy concentrating on cost reduction or performance improvement to notice the warning signs or understand the relationship between their teams' behaviour and the demands of the job.

In some other organisations – unfortunately, in our experience, far too many – some managers turn a blind eye to stress at work. They don't look because they don't want to see. Acknowledging that stress exists forces them to deal with the issues. In the most severe case of this that we have seen, a senior manager refused an opportunity for his division to participate in a stress audit on the grounds that he knew with certainty that issues would be uncovered that would place the business in the position where they would be obliged to do something about it. Thus, this manager reasoned, it would be more prudent not to start the investigation in the first place. The fact that the cost of not acting was considerably in excess of the cost of dealing with the issues somehow escaped his notice. As we predicted, this manager's state of blissful denial didn't last long. The combination of poor performance, high absence, excessive staff turnover and threats of legal action forced him to raise his head from the sand and do something. Unfortunately the awareness came too late. For a great many other people, the idea of getting to grips with the real issues and really understanding the effects of the problem is just too hard. As one senior manager said, 'It's in that box over there marked "difficult".'

Whether or not managers want to formally look for the effects, and how much detail they want to go into, the organisational signs and symptoms are there to be seen. To the trained eye they are blindingly obvious.

THREE

The Cost of Stress

Stress matters because it damages people. And they in turn damage the organisations that they work for. However much argument there may be about definitions of stress, what it is and what it is not, we know and can observe that there are times when people are made ill by the psychosocial demands of their workplaces. We know how this mechanism works and we know that we have a moral, financial, and legal responsibility to do something about it. The problems arise when we try to quantify the extent of the damage, and the extent of our responsibility. We shall be examining the issues of responsibility in a later chapter. This chapter and the next are concerned with deepening our understanding of the human and commercial consequences of workplace stress and helping us to recognise the organisational signs and symptoms.

Most organisations should be able to identify that they have potential stress issues. They can observe some signs within their organisation that would suggest they might have a problem. Only a small number, however, will be able to fully describe the likely consequences of any of their problems. This is because they look the other way. They focus on issues such as performance, change, products, services; in effect they look over the heads of other people to outcomes, and ignore the people who produce those outcomes. Many of the signs are not immediately apparent at the organisational level. As a result there is generally more uncertainty about the organisational effects of stress, i.e. by how much and in what way the damage to the people damages the organisation.

This lack of understanding is significant, as it is often responsible for the apathy shown by many organisations towards addressing workplace stress in a proactive way. What gets measured gets managed, and many of the organisational behaviours that are affected by stress fall outside of 'standard' management accounting. These are what we can call 'invisible' costs and we will be looking at them more closely in Chapter 4.

A proactive approach to stress

In the previous chapter, we described ways in which you can identify some of the more easily recognisable signs that indicate that a stress problem exists. Our aim in doing this is twofold.

1. First, we want to raise awareness of how much valuable information already exists within companies to help assess whether there is a problem with workplace stress. With a deeper understanding of the relationship between stress and some of the metrics routinely used in business, it is possible to look at your existing information in a new way that provides real clues about the way pressure affects your staff.

2. The second objective relates to the first. In our experience, it is rare for one person within an organisation to be able to champion the cause of a proactive approach to stress management. The enlightened stakeholder needs support from their colleagues in order to deal with stress effectively. The best way of gaining support is to present the *evidence* that a problem exists and that the problem translates to hard *financial* costs as well as human ones.

If organisations really understood the cost to their business of employee stress they would invest much more time and resources in managing the effects of pressure. In our experience once they do know the cost, once they have the evidence, a more robust commitment to action quickly follows. The evidence is all around you but most people don't see it. You need to turn the light on to find the metaphorical bodies on the floor. But first you need to look for the light switches!

To quantify the extent of this damage we should look at two significant strands of loss: the commercial costs and the human costs. As has already been said, some of these are easy to see and some are less obvious.

The commercial costs

Sickness absence

A lot has been written about sickness absence in recent years, and during this time there has been a growing understanding of the role stress plays in driving absence behaviours. The emphasis though should be placed on 'growing understanding', for in our experience there are still a surprising number of organisations that have not accepted the relationship between the two.

A brief look at most attendance management conference agendas would suggest that a good many companies still hold the view that employees take time off work for one of only two reasons. They are either genuinely physically ill – in which case 'get well soon and please hurry up and come back' – or they are 'malingering'. 'Professional advice' in this area is often therefore still focused on case-managing the long-term sick back to work and inventing robust monitoring systems to 'catch out' the malingerers by tighter control.

Why employees might actually want to 'malinger' is rarely challenged. This behaviour is accepted as normal, albeit undesirable, and simply needs to be controlled by tighter policing of frequent short-term absence. There is rarely any thought given to whether a legitimate reason exists *why* the person might not want to come to work. There is an attitude of 'if there is nothing physically wrong with you then you must be workshy'.

That this attitude still prevails is interesting to us because – in all the work we have done with companies, helping them to understand the dynamics of the relationship between their employees and their workplace – we found almost no evidence of malingering. We have worked with many thousands of workers, both in the UK and abroad, from shop floor to top floor. We have met plenty of people who felt themselves unable to go to work; very very few have deliberately set out to take advantage of the company, but they have a different story to tell. Unlike the behaviour attributable to the 'malingerer mentality' the individuals taking these absence days are more likely to be suffering from a surfeit of commitment than a shortage of it. They are more likely to be creaking from trying to do too much than yawning with boredom, or are more likely to be struggling with a difficult relationship at work than struggling to be bothered to get out of bed. Normal attendance behaviour is to attend, not to stay away. Employees who do not attend on a regular basis always have a reason not to do so – it just may not be what you think it is!

It seems then that in most cases 'malingerer' turns out to be the most inappropriate of labels. The term implies laziness, a lack of willingness to expend effort and a lack of commitment. In our experience the percentage of people who actually possess these characteristics in a workforce is very small – certainly considerably smaller than the number of employees who are absent at any one time attributed to non-physical complaints. What accounts then for the gap?

The answer is simple. The bulk of the gap is made up of literally thousands of employees who are under-recognised, under-supported, ignored, overburdened or bored. Many of them don't come to work because they can't face another day – they would like to but they just do not think they can cope with the experience. Some of them, it is true, don't want to go to work because they can see no good reason to – they get nothing out of the workplace except the money, and the money is not the motivator. But that does not make them a malingerer. In our experience most want to be in work and are happy to exchange their time for money, but they want also to get some form of fulfilment out of their role – some sense of being appreciated for the contribution they have made, however big or small.

Failure to meet the most basic human needs in the workplace – such as support, recognition, influence and control – is a massive contributor to employee stress and one of the key reasons that stress is highly correlated with absence. It is also the reason why some companies still cannot see the relationship. Stress is not just about being overburdened. We tend to see stress and overwork as synonyms but they are not. Stress occurs when pressures combine in a way to out-strip an individual's capacity to deal with them. If an employee has a need for recognition and does not get any (or worse gets recognised only when a mistake is made), then this is as stressful for them as being overburdened is to the worker with too much to do and too little time to do it in.

Employees will struggle with these situations for just so long before they start taking time off. Frequent short-term absences don't often come from people who are clinically ill psychologically; the people we might more readily think of as 'stressed out' and needing time to recover. These unlucky few are off work for long periods of time and, in some cases, never return to work. The other, more common, stress absences are the one-off short-term absences that eventually, if there is no cessation in the pressures, become frequent short-term absences. For a subset of these people the issues will become more severe and so frequent short-term absence becomes a smaller number of longer spells of absence. In turn some of those cases will eventually become long-term absence. The way stress absence cases develop is predictable, and if your systems and the quality of your data is good enough you may be able to interrog-ate your own company's absence data and identify patterns of progression.

So stress plays a key role in short- and long-term absence behaviour and may be the single biggest cause of frequent short-term absence, particularly those days less easily attributable to observable physical illness. But stress may also be a factor in many of the absences that *are* due to these physical complaints.

The biggest cause of absence in the UK is musculo-skeletal conditions, with lower back pain being the most common of these. Together with stress-related absence these account for 80% of lost working days. Stress is now known to be a contributory factor in the development of some musculo-skeletal complaints and certainly has a role in the capacity of individuals to effectively manage their condition.

Very many employees will have on-going muscle and joint problems, which they have learnt to live with and manage the effects of. Stress affects this group too because capacity to cope with pain is significantly influenced by the mental attitude of the individual. When workplace pressure becomes too much, the capacity to deal effectively with the underlying condition is reduced. When this happens the likely result is an absence or a more prolonged absence. There is a growing body of evidence to suggest that the length of time people take off work with back pain is highly dependent on their attitude and beliefs about back pain. These attitudes and beliefs are affected by their morale and their emotional commitment to the workplace.

Stress also plays a significant part in the rate at which employees take time off for 'common complaints' like colds and stomach upsets. The effect of constant adrenalisation on the body is now much better understood, in particular the action that it has on the immune system. Employees suffering from stress and taking lots of "sickies" are often quite genuinely sick. Immune system depletion brought about by constant adrenalisation means that stressed employees really are more susceptible to the invasion of bacteria and viruses. Many of the colds and flu that appear in the sickness data are therefore genuine physical absence with stress-related causes. Similarly stress is a factor in very many other physical complaints, amongst them skin disorders, musculo-skeletal complaints and gastrointestinal dysfunction.

It should now be clear that, across the workplace, stress is likely to be the single biggest driver for sickness absence. Difficulty in getting organisations to understand the relationship has hitherto been due to a lack of understanding about the way stress affects employee health, as well as difficulties in understanding exactly what absence information can tell you. Many of the stress-related causes of absence discussed in this chapter will appear in absence data cloaked in the physical effects or outcomes of the problem, rather than by direct reference to stress itself. This has much to do with the taboo that historically surrounds stress in the workplace. 'Stress' is often available as a reason for absence in data coding but, given the stigma attached to a diagnosis of stress, such a reason for absence is rarely given. This deliberate misrepresentation of the reason for absence is invariably explained by employee fear that admitting to stress is likely to lead, at best, to being overlooked for promotion, at worst to being a candidate at the next round of redundancies. So, instead of being accurately reported, these absences bulk out all other more acceptable reasons for absence, the colds, flu, migraine and stomach disorders. However, once you have started to really look and think about the patterns in your absence data, the more likely reasons can reveal themselves. Never doubt the power of absence data as a temperature check for the wellbeing of the workforce – it is arguably the most easily read data that you have on your doorstep.

Now that we have established that a relationship exists, what does it cost? Estimates vary wildly as to the actual cost of stress-related absence but all the numbers given are huge. Calculating the direct cost of salary for absent workers is the most commonly used measure and at current UK rates of absence and salary this, according to the annual CBI survey on sickness absence, is equivalent to around £6 billion per annum countrywide. At a local company level, a firm with average levels of sickness absence is probably losing the equivalent of 3% of annual turnover. We should remind ourselves too that we are counting only the direct costs of salary and temporary staff. As we shall see in the next chapter, the indirect costs associated with stress absence are huge too, and will almost certainly be equal to or even greater than the direct costs.

Fortunately, in order to estimate the cost of stress from your absence data you don't have to question every sick note or even delve on an individual basis into the underlying reasons for absence. Remember that at this stage you are probably just collecting high-level evidence and developing your hypothesis to gain support for a more detailed investigation. Make your own judgement about the proportion of short-term absence that you think may be linked to pressure from work. Is it 50%, 75% or 90%?

To help calculate this percentage, think about our experience of working with a large call centre where understanding the relationship between stress and absence behaviour gave a clear illustration of the direct cost to the company of stress causing extended absence. In this call centre absence rates were running at almost 20% – a huge cost to a growing business where the number of available customer service agents was directly linked to the ability to satisfy customer demand. When we investigated absence and stress we found, amongst other factors, a simple relationship between number of days off and the attitude of the supervisor. In essence the supervisors were making the 'return to work' interviews so unpleasant for the staff that an absent employee would extend their absence in order to delay their interview. If they could extend a one-day absence into a week by persuading their GP to provide a sick note, then so much the better. Think about two factors when calculating the impact of stress:

1. Is there anything that may make an employee decide it's better to stay at home than come to work? – the decision to take time off.
2. Is there anything that may make an employee prefer to stay at home rather than return to work? – the decision to delay the return to work.

If something at work prompts an employee to take a day off or extend the length of time they are absent, then your organisation is paying a price for poor wellbeing. You decide just how big that number is in your workplace.

Absence, however, is not the only price the organisation can pay – there are other equally costly penalties.

Litigation

A major and growing direct cost to companies is the cost of legal action taken against them by employees who can prove personal injury as a result of pressure at work. These costs include the pay-outs to employees who are able to bring a successful case against their employer, the fines imposed for breaking the law, the time taken up by managers and staff in preparing and defending a case and, of course, the legal fees.

The direct cost of litigation is therefore easy to account for and the sums are getting larger as the number of successful cases rises. Back in 1995 the case of John Walker vs Northumberland County Council grabbed the headlines with the then record pay-out of £175 000. Although Walker vs Northumberland County Council was by no means the first, it was seen at the time as a landmark case that would 'open the floodgates' for a great many other cases. Since that time the number of cases hitting the headlines has grown enormously. In July 1999, Beverly Lancaster, a former housing officer, was awarded £67 000 damages against Birmingham City Council as compensation for the stress she suffered following a job transfer. In October 1999 there were further reports of stress-related compensation when a teacher, Muriel Benson, won £47 000 for stress-related illness caused by overwork. In May 2000 another teacher known as Mr A was awarded £300 000 damages in an out-of-court settlement for stress-related illness.

These headline grabbing cases and settlements are only the tip of the iceberg. Headline stories feature only the big money pay-outs or the more 'newsworthy' stories. Many more claims go unreported or are settled out of court. In fact in the UK the *Independent on Sunday* reported that claims for compensation due to stress are the leading reason for unions taking cases to courts and tribunals. As a result it is currently estimated that there are over 3000 stress-related claims at some stage in the litigation process

Litigation is expensive, not just because of the financial burden of substantial damages and legal fees but also through the more indirect cost of the time spent defending cases and damage to the brand and public relations. The increasingly frequent settlements continue to demonstrate that employers simply cannot afford to ignore the effects of stress on their workforce if they want to avoid these costs.

Employer liability

The costs of employee legal actions are usually further compounded by the way in which employer liability (EL) insurance premiums are calculated. There is usually a straight-line relationship between the number and value of claims made against EL insurance and the subsequent year's insurance premiums. The increasing risk burden for underwriters from the growing number of successful stress claims is significant and one which they cannot absorb. The average cost of an EL claim is around £5000 inclusive of cost and expenses – compensation payouts of over £100 000 for stress cases are becoming more common and that is without the expenses and costs. You can do the maths yourself. Employers with a claims history from stress cases can expect dramatically increased premiums. The more claims you have, or the more costly the claims become, the higher premium underwriters will charge.

Staff turnover

Along with sickness absence, high rates of staff turnover are one of the clearest organisational signs of stress. The relationship between the issue and the metric is simple. People who are made ill by their work, who can't cope with the pressures of their job or who find the employment unfulfilling, will leave if they are able to find alternative work. In a period of relatively full employment, few people will stay if they don't have to. The direct cost of attrition is high and anyone who leaves a company, that the organisation doesn't want to lose, represents a cost significantly in excess of the cost of recruiting a replacement.

If the cost of missed opportunities, reduction of service levels and training of a replacement is also taken into account then the true cost of attrition represents a significant drain on company resources. Time and time again, we see organisations pouring hundreds of thousands of pounds into recruitment and training programmes only to see this entire investment leak away as existing personnel walk out of the revolving door, frequently into similar roles with competitors. In some organisations the cost of unwanted attrition means that money spent on managing pressure will result in a massive and speedy return on investment. For example, one of our clients had an annual attrition rate of 21% in their call centres. Implementing improvements to manage pressure and improve wellbeing helped reduce this figure to 15% in a year. With average recruitment and retraining costs at thousands of pounds per employee the payback period for them was measured in weeks!

The cost of staff turnover becomes even more dramatic when the impact on the loss of human or intellectual capital is taken into account. The true market value of the knowledge that employees leave with – the intellectual property – is almost incalculable. Likewise the individual bundle of experience and insight that they brought to the workplace with them each day is not immediately, if ever, truly replicable in a new member of staff. When good people leave you are losing intellectual capital and as Thomas Stewart the author of the groundbreaking book *Intellectual Capital* says, 'Intellectual capital – not natural resources, machinery or even financial capital – has become the one indispensable asset of corporations.' The cost of attrition is very high indeed.

It is worth remembering at this point that pressure itself is not necessarily correlated with high staff turnover. It is a simple mistake to make, particularly in companies where high staff turnover is accepted as the norm because (sic) 'this is a highly pressurised environment'. Remember: pressure does not have to lead to stress. Some work environments – for example, call centres – can be highly pressurised; we might describe the work here as 'inherently stressful'. Yet we meet companies with these working conditions who report lower turnover than some traditionally 'less stressful' jobs. Why might this be? The answer is simple. Turnover does not have to be a feature of pressurised environments if the pressure is managed appropriately. Obviously part of getting it right means recruiting the right people for the work environment, but that is not the entire story as we will see in the next chapter. Employees who experience workplace pressure as a positive stimulus that encour-ages personal growth and leads to fulfilment in their work are far less likely to look for other jobs. They will find it much easier to resist the temptation when a higher salary for a similar role appears in the newspaper. Pressure that is appropriate for the individual can lead to growth and fulfilment in the role and robust commitment for the organisation. These are all diametric opposites of the behaviours that lead to the exit interview!

Accidents

Accidents, like absence and staff turnover, are another easy-to-measure consequence of stress at work. Not all accidents are stress-related but very many, perhaps the majority, have a stress component. There is a growing appreciation that accidents happen more often to employees who experience stress on a long-term basis.

The direct cost of an accident is obvious: the time taken to deal with it; the absence from work; damage done to plant, machinery and stock; compensation payments and the corresponding insurance loading. An employer liability underwriter calculated that a company with 13 lost time accidents resulting in nine claims lost 520 working days and paid out £5172 per claim. However, when they added operator costs, lost production, medical costs and the costs of investigation to the settlement, the total bill was £171 000 or £19 000 per claim. In this example the company concluded that they needed to increase sales by £3 million to cover these costs and maintain the expected profit level.

A simple analysis of the causes of accidents and an estimate of the extent to which human error is a factor will give an indication of the size of the problem. The link to stress is straightforward. What was it that caused the mistake to be made? Why would someone who's worked safely for years suddenly get it wrong? Were they distracted or preoccupied? Had they been showing signs of fatigue? Did they feel it was all getting too much? Most accident reporting focuses on what happened and takes little notice of the mental state of the employee at the time. If the accident is due to so called 'human error' there is a strong argument to support the view that a significant proportion of this is due to stress. Stress explains the failure to observe safe working practices because an employee hasn't got time to do the job properly or the pressing of the wrong button because the employee is preoccupied with an argument at home. The costs when this happens can be significant.

The importance of invisible costs

So far, we have looked at the obvious effects of stress at an organisational level and at some of the ways the associated costs can be calculated. However, in some organisations the indirect costs of stress – such as poor quality or productivity – may provide a better insight into the prevalence of stress-related ill health than some of the more obvious direct costs – such as staff turnover or absence. Although levels of unemployment are generally quite low we have seen some organisations operating in pockets of high unemployment where getting a different job isn't an easy option. Some of these organisations may also have strictly enforced rules for controlling sickness absence with severe penalties to force people to come to work. If absence is controlled too tightly then people will come to work when they shouldn't. They become the 'presentees' – the people who are there in body but certainly not in mind. These are the people who make mistakes, jeopardise quality and have accidents. The sickness absence figures may look good but other metrics would show serious cause for concern. In these cases neither absence nor staff turnover are good indicators of stress levels within the organisation. The management can point to the data as evidence that they are good employers – 'People don't leave and they don't go sick therefore we are doing all right'. But they would be drawing the wrong conclusions.

These people are the lowest-cost evangelists; they discount or ignore the cost of health. They don't think they have a problem, they don't realise that it is the goodwill of the staff, the skills of managers, the professional ability of the human resources (HR) or occupational health departments (OH) that is covering up the cracks in the organisation. In the proactive world of employee health, success is marked by a non-event.

If we turn our attention to some other measures – such as quality or customer satisfaction – we might see a different picture. Stress at work will show up somewhere. Poor decision-making and loss of concentration will have an effect on every aspect of work and there will be consequences. The next chapter deals with what these could be.

FOUR

What Effect Does Stress Have on Performance and Productivity?

The invisible costs

So far we have looked at the most obvious organisational signs of stress and their attendant costs. But, as Figure 4.1 shows, the true cost to the organisation is very much greater than the direct costs.

We need to look below the surface because, in many respects, stress in the workplace does the most damage commercially when it is least easy to see. As we described in the previous chapter, stress absences do not begin as a long-term absence. They are usually preceded by several periods of short-term absence. Likewise someone who is suffering from stress does not take days off straight away. A period of time elapses when they are effectively invisible in the

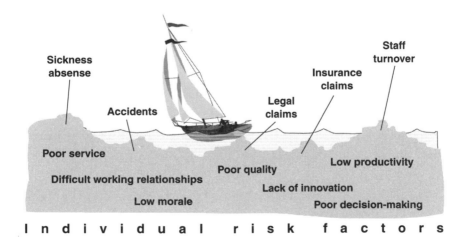

Figure 4.1   *The visible and invisible costs of stress*

workplace, apparently getting on with the business to the best of their ability. They do not become noticeable until they have become absent. But before they went off sick they were talking to customers, making decisions, making product. The reality will have been that during this period they were extremely unlikely to be performing at their best. The chances are that nobody will have noticed. What's the cost to your business of the cumulative effect of underperformance?

In the modern downsized workplace we ask our employees to give their all. Not only do our production schedules depend on our employees consistently contributing on a practical level at a very high rate, but we also require them to think, plan, create, innovate and delight all those that they come into contact with. The paradox is that whilst businesses presuppose and budget for this level of contribution, the scant regard given for our employees as they attempt to deliver all of this means that we often create an environment where it is impossible to contribute at the required level for more than a short period. Put more simply – we need our employees to perform at a level that is so demanding we ensure that we will not get what we need. Why is this so? When employees get stressed they become literally incapable of behaving in a way that will produce the commercial outputs we need to successfully compete. Modern businesses need continuous improvement in productivity, efficiency, quality, customer service, innovation and creativity. This means employees need to be consistently alert, committed, engaged, focused and fulfilled as well as supported and recognised by their managers. We know from our work with employees that they are unable to feel all of those things all of the time and we definitely know that they are rarely supported and recognised in the same proportion that these demands are made of them. When the demands are high and support is low the stress reaction kicks in and creativity, innovation and so on is a physical as well as an emotional impossibility.

There is then a fundamental relationship to be understood between employee wellbeing, their motivation and their performance.

Wellbeing, motivation and performance

At any one point of time, every one of us occupies a space some-where along a notional continuum that runs from ill heath through to fulfilment. Some people are made ill by their work and some are fulfilled by it. The number at the extremes is small, with the majority of people being somewhere in the middle (see Figure 4.2).

Where people sit on the continuum is something of a movable feast. Events will occur in the course of a person's employment to move them temporarily in either direction and this is to be expected. However, it is the role that pressure and stress can play in accelerating an employee's movement one way or another along the continuum that interests us here. Pressure, when it is appropriate to an individual's capacity to cope, can be a major stimulus for personal growth and development and therefore increases the chances of people feeling fulfilled in their work. Conversely, when pressure turns to stress the progression turns rapidly away from fulfilment towards ill health. As we have seen, if stress is prolonged, this transition can be very rapid indeed.

Where employees are on this continuum is important for a number of reasons. It is self-evident that employees should not be made ill by their work and so there are legal and humanitarian imperatives why we want our employees to keep away from this end of the spectrum. But it is worth recognising that each stage along the continuum represents a break point in energy, enthusiasm, creativity, innovation and motivation. While there will be exceptions to the rule, the closer employees are to fulfilment the greater the chances of them being able to deliver all the subtle innovations and creative ideas your business needs to survive.

One of the least observable but most dangerous costs to the business is the loss of creativity and innovation that happens when employees move away from fulfilment and toward the left of this continuum.

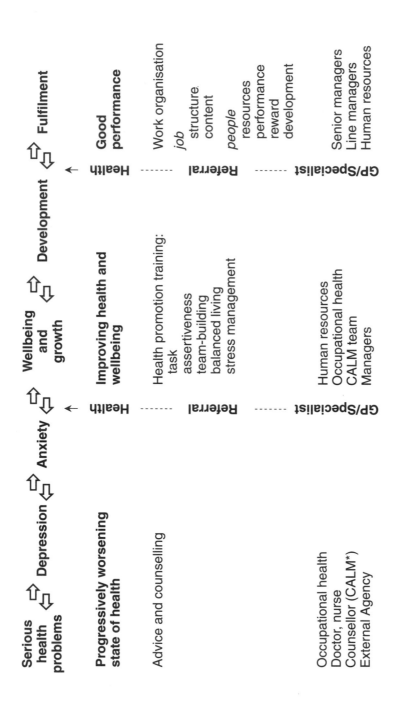

Figure 4.2 *The ill health to fulfilment continuum*

*CALM – Counselling and Life Management.

Source: R. J. Heron and E. L. Teasdale. Reproduced by permission of AstraZeneca.

Creativity and innovation

As has already been said, modern businesses require continuous improvement across all their activities. We need all our people, not just our managers, to be innovative and creative in their approach in order to propel the incremental improvement in product and service that drives success in the market place. In some sectors, like the pharmaceutical industry, their very future depends on a small number of employees making the breakthrough connection in the laboratories that will lead to the next world-class drug. We take this creativity and innovation for granted, but we shouldn't.

One of the clearest illustrations of the effect of pressure on performance is the impact on creativity and innovation. We know that some pressure can be stimulating and can act as a prompt for significant creative insights. People can come up with original and innovative solutions when they are put in a difficult situation, when something breaks or when the deadline is only minutes away and an answer needs to be found. The phrase 'necessity is the mother of invention' reminds us that sometimes the chemical changes that occur during the first phase of the stress reaction act to sharpen the mind and focus all our attention on the problem at hand. We move into a zone where the ideas flow and the barrier that has held us paralysed and unable to act is blown away. That is the positive link between pressure and stress – a short-term stimulus that releases our creative energy.

Unfortunately there is another, much more damaging reaction. This occurs when pressure leads to stress, when the demands placed upon us exceed our ability to cope. This is the phase where our bodies and minds are no longer thriving on pressure but are starting to shut down. We are tired and listless, energy levels are low and sometimes we think that it's all too much effort. In this state we dwell on the problems, focus on our weaknesses and find it almost impossible to think clearly about anything. There is no creativity or innovation, no room for original thought. We go through the motions of our daily lives operating on autopilot with as little reference to the world outside our problems as possible. This is the situation found in many organisations where stress is endemic. There is very little creativity, people dislike change and new ideas are either ignored or devalued.

Predictably this lack of creativity and innovation has a major impact on the effectiveness of the organisation. Tired, anxious people who dislike their jobs are not going to produce the next technical breakthrough, the new wonder drug or killer software application. On a more prosaic level they will not be the people who find an innovative way to solve a customer's problem or track down a missing delivery or even work out how to use the headings feature of the word-processor! The cost of stress in terms of reduced creativity and innovation isn't only a problem for people working in R&D or design; it affects every employee in the business whose ideas can make a difference to efficiency and organisational success, and that is every single person in the organisation!

Competitive advantage

The damage that stress does to creativity and innovation is linked to the impact on competitive advantage. In a world where knowledge is king and organisations are beginning to place a financial value on the intellectual capital of the business, it is clear that a stressed workforce cannot be a competitive workforce. Companies increasingly differ- entiate themselves from their competitors by the quality of their service. In most cases at least, it is human beings who deliver this service and so the quality of customer experience is going to be linked very closely to the quality of the contacts and relation- ships that they have with the people who work there. This is self- evident – but despite this companies have been slow to recognise the impact of a stressed employee on the overall customer experi- ence. Employees who, for whatever reason, feel themselves over- burdened and under-recognised cannot deliver the same quality of service as the employee who feels recognised, supported and fulfilled by their work.

If people are an organisation's most important asset then their contribution needs to be recognised and valued accordingly. Even the most hard-edged and ruthless businesses must realise that it doesn't make commercial sense to damage a major asset. Neither does it make sense to develop a strategy that focuses on damage limitation. Instead, organisations need to recognise that stress drains the creative energy and collective contribution of the workforce. In these times of slimmer and leaner workforces, creating environments that will facilitate the greatest contribution from each employee should be as much a part of the objective as reducing the number of times they are damaged. The paybacks are there – for competitive advantage lives or dies in the wellbeing of the workforce.

Poor decision-making

The loss of creativity and innovation is not the only way that stress dulls the mind. The stress reaction causes people to doubt their abilities and to fail to take sufficient notice of what goes on around them. This can lead to errors in decision-making. Fight or flight aren't the only way to react to a threat; we can also freeze.

Freezing in response to a threat can take many forms; we can stay immobilised, unable to do anything, even think. We see this when anxiety overwhelms a speaker or a performer and they stop in mid-sentence, completely unable to go on. We also see it when someone is faced with a difficult decision, perhaps one that requires something as simple as a yes-or-no reply, and they break down with their inability to choose. The other reaction, the opposite end of the scale is when people rush around in panic. They avoid having to make a decision by creating a whirlwind of ineffectual activity. All action but no direction.

These dysfunctional responses to a threat shape the everyday lives of people struggling to manage the complexities of today's workplace. We are faced with a bewildering array of choices: about what to do, where to go, who to see, what to buy, how to get there, what to say, how to tell someone, whose advice to take, and so on. With the increasing complexity of technology at work and a growing tendency to encourage job autonomy and individual discretion, more and more people are required to spend more and more time making decisions. Stress matters in this context because the quality of the decision-making deteriorates when pressure exceeds people's ability to cope. As we've seen, the initial immediate reaction to a threat may sharpen our critical faculties but that soon turns into sensory overload or psychological disengagement.

Once again stress can cause a malfunction at two ends of the scale. We can be so overloaded with thoughts, ideas and choices that we lose the ability to discriminate. We are under pressure to perform, to do something, so we make a choice without really thinking through the consequences or giving the decision the time it deserves. Under those circumstances it's not surprising that we make mistakes. We become distracted, our attention span decreases, we get frustrated, but we have to make a decision before we can move on to the next urgent job. When we're in this situation we find ourselves having to make a decision, any decision! It may not be a very good one but at least we've got one less thing to worry about and we can get on with panicking about the next meeting.

For other people, the process is different; there are too many decisions to make, too much information to absorb, too many people to talk to. They find they can't cope any more so they start to switch off. They lose interest. They can't be bothered to think about the situation, don't care about the outcome and procrastinate for as long as possible. This disassociation from the workplace cripples the decision-making process and creates a working environment with a 'couldn't care less' attitude to service, quality and performance. There is no energy and no commitment, just indifference.

Employee goodwill

Another important invisible cost is the erosion over time of employee goodwill towards the company. The value of employee goodwill is hard to quantify in terms of the contribution it makes to company success, particularly during periods of rapid or uncomfortable change. Many companies unconsciously trade on it – introducing unpopular practices and policies that staff won't like but will 'bear with us' on. The fact remains though, and of course this point is linked to the previous section, goodwill is a finite currency – once you have spent it there is no more to be had.

The burden of suffering caused is a cost to the employee and one that is not so easy for the employer to measure. Employees who are repeatedly ill, whether or not they attribute their ill health to the demands of the workplace, will slowly become drained of energy and enthusiasm. By way of an analogy, a favoured garment can be repeatedly dry-cleaned and retextured at a specialist cleaner, but each time it comes back, perhaps imperceptibly at first, the lustre of the material will have faded. The employee rests and recovers and returns to the workplace, effectively surface-cleaned, but the causes of the stress are most probably still there and a return to ill health is often only a matter of time. The cycle of decline and recovery revolves again and the employee returns to work for a second, third, fourth time. Each time though he is likely to be just a little more diminished than the last time.

This slow erosion of lustre is not limited to the employee. The effect is likely to be the same for members of the employee's family. Companies like AstraZeneca, who are very proactive in the area of wellbeing management, have recognised the contribution that supportive families make to the sustained high performance of their employees. These companies make a point of formally acknowledging, wherever they can, the role that's been played in supporting the employed family member through periods of change and uncertainty. Those employees who are fortunate enough to return to a supportive family or even social environment are, whether they are aware of it or not, effectively cleaned up after work. Of course, under different circumstances the complete opposite can be true! However, when they co-exist well together functional family environments can offer a retreat and contrast from the demands of the workplace. When life balance is good or partner tolerance high, there is an opportunity to unwind and put the problems of the workplace in perspective.

Likewise when employees are ill, a supportive family environment offers 'a safe house' in which to rest and recuperate. But families can lose patience when one of them is repeatedly injured. Families by and large have no experience of the employee's life in work. They base their affection and enjoyment of the person on how they experience them at home and in a social rather than a commercial setting. Tolerance of the employers' wish to trade their partners' time and expertise for salary diminishes, if an additional part of the deal appears to be that the employee is too tired or unwell to participate in family life on a regular basis. In a survey recently published by the CIPD, 'Married to the Job' it is reported that one in three partners of people who work more than 48 hours in a typical week, say the additional time spent at work has a negative effect on their personal relationship. Over 50% of all partners interviewed felt that the long hours worked by their partner affected the physical side of their relationship and 70% of those interviewed felt that their partner was frequently too tired to hold a conversation. The survey goes on to report that 43% felt fed up with shouldering the bulk of the domestic burden, and two-fifths of those interviewed felt that working long hours has resulted in arguments with their spouse or partner.

What happens in practical terms, when home life is affected in this way, is that family goodwill and support for the employer starts to be withdrawn. You might think this does not matter. After all, the employer has a contract with the employee not the whole family. But it does matter. When we employ a person the whole person comes to work, not just the bit that does the job. The background circumstances of our employee's lives influence the quality of their work. If we want them to go the extra mile it matters even more, because to go the extra mile they may need to prevail upon the goodwill of another family member. When families withdraw their support the employee has to go out on a limb. If support and commitment for the employer remains high they may decide to placate at home and carry on 'putting their arm in the fire', safe in the knowledge they will now have to lick the wounds better themselves. Or they could stop what they are doing and find another job. In either of these scenarios who loses? In both of them it is always somebody – the employee, the employer, or the family.

The human costs of stress are therefore more far-reaching than we might at first think. The reason whole lives are affected by it is that it is impossible to separate the employee from his environment, however hard some employees might try to do this for themselves in the relentless pursuit of their corporate objectives! It is the unique cocktail of individual life experiences, attitudes and beliefs that makes each employee valuable. It is this same unique combination of external influences and responsibilities that can make him so vulnerable too. The employer has little chance of knowing the details of the landscape that his employee occupies outside of the workplace. In most respects this is all as it should be. The employer does, however, need to constantly remind himself that a life does exist and that the choices we make in corporations in terms of what we ask people to do affect others outside of the workplace just as surely as what happens outside of work affects what goes on inside. The employer does not have to know which colours and features are on the canvas but he does have to know that a broader picture exists.

Mistakes

People make mistakes, but people who are stressed make more of them. The mistake, as we've seen, may lead to an accident or it may lead to lost production, unacceptable quality, or a fundamentally flawed strategy for the whole organisation. When mistakes are made at this level then the associated costs might not be immediately observable. That does not, however, make them any less real.

The situation is complicated by the fact that in our modern service-led economy the mistakes are just as likely to be intellectual as practical. Either way, they can have far-reaching implications and significant costs for the business.

Quality

The impact of stress on quality is easy to observe. The combination of lack of involvement, poor decision-making and a 'couldn't care less' attitude leads inevitably to problems with quality. Much has been written about the cost of quality and the relationship between quality levels and organisational success. Improving the quality of an organisation's products and services has been a major strategic objective for many years and has done much to improve systems and change attitudes. Businesses have made a huge investment in designing quality systems and developing a quality culture; however, they will fail to gain the full benefit of their quality programmes unless they also reduce stress.

It is ironic that some of the basic principles of quality management apply to products but not to people. Faulty machines are replaced, systems that damage the goods are redesigned, and every effort is made to improve quality at source, to design it into the system from the beginning. This is not the case with employees. The emphasis is on rejecting the failures or providing remedial help rather than creating a workplace that promotes employees' wellbeing.

Dealing with stress in this way is exactly the same as managing quality by having an inspection line where faulty goods are rejected. Actually, it's worse because in most inspection lines some effort is made to find out why the rejected goods failed the quality standard. Patterns are identified and, in all but the worst-run companies, some effort is made to find and fix the cause of the reject. With people suffering from stress, one of the most basic principles of good quality management – control quality at source – seems to be ignored.

Linking the cost of quality to the management of stress focuses attention on employee wellbeing as a major determinant of the success of a quality programme and it helps people to realise the financial benefits of getting it right.

Low productivity and profitability

In the same way that we use quality as a way of putting a distance between our competitors and ourselves, we also seek to differentiate ourselves by our ability to produce goods and services at a better or cheaper rate. Constant improvement is now hard-wired into all performance management. If we are not getting better we will be going backwards. Therefore we need our teams to meet ever-tighter production schedules and we need more, of a better product, faster but with the same or increased profit margin. No mean feat and one that employees are able to achieve surprisingly often – which only goes to show how much capacity employees have for incremental performance improvement.

It is in reducing the level of individual employee potential, however, that organisational stress leaves another imprint on the organisation. In the same way that stress undermines employees' ability to think creatively, make good decisions, deliver quality and so on, so it drastically reduces ability and motivation to perform to a high standard. This is key. Stress lowers the performance of every single employee who experiences it – not just those who are suffering from extreme stress. Every employee with stress issues, even if these are not disabling, is performing below their level of ability. The harsh reality of organisational life is that stress drives underachievement.

Pressure and Performance

Figure 4.3 illustrates the relationship between pressure and performance; it describes the link between the demands that people face and the extent to which these demands have positive, negative or neutral outcomes.

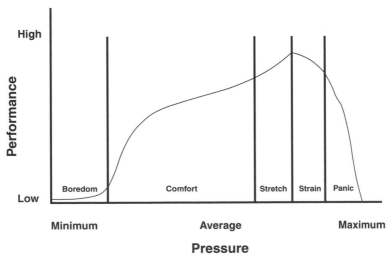

Figure 4.3 *Pressure performance curve*

Figure 4.3 suggests, as we have said elsewhere, that we all need some pressure in our lives. If we remove pressure, if we remove stimulus, then we get into the phase of boredom or rust-out. This is what happens to people who are in very undemanding jobs, particularly those with little control and lots of repetitive work.

Most people prefer to operate with some, but not too much pressure. This area is called the 'comfort zone'. There are some challenges, but we're comfortable with our ability to cope with them. When pressure increases and we're asked to do a little bit more than we're comfortable with or we're used to doing, then we get into what we call our 'stretch zone'. This is where we're being pushed beyond our comfort level. The limits are being extended, the boundaries are moving. But as we find additional resources and meet the challenge, so performance tends to increase. The threat we have to watch out for is when the pressures continue to increase and we start to find ourselves hanging on by our fingertips. We're just about managing but we realise we're really not coping too well. We have moved into the 'strain zone' where we start seeing physical signs and feeling some physical symptoms of anxiety.

When pressure continues to increase, or when our ability to cope begins to fail, we find ourselves in the 'panic zone'. This is the major risk, and it can happen very quickly. We drop off the edge; we simply can't cope any more. This is when people are unable to deal with the situation and start to experience major problems. As the curve demonstrates, performance will decline very rapidly and these people will soon become clinically ill.

The graph serves to remind us that people in the panic zone should be the priority for concern and support. But it also reminds us that they are not the only people whose performance is affected and about whom we should be concerned. The effect for all individuals who have been working at a level beyond their capacity to cope is that depleting energy and increasing fatigue eventually slows productivity and performance – despite attempts by the individual to maintain their output. Once out of the stretch zone, and into the strain zone, productivity declines. Employees may manage to convince themselves and those around them that the volume of work is the same and that targets are being met, but in practice performance will be lower. This has huge cost implications for any organisation trying to differentiate itself on service, quality, price or product. That therefore means every company. But there is a greater cost still.

The role of discretionary effort

Perhaps the most significant, yet least reported, cost of stress is lost opportunity. This is the opportunity to release even a small proportion of the additional performance potential that is locked inside every employee and not yet released into the business. All employees have extra capacity they could give – if they wanted to. If companies knew more about the effect of pressure on their employees – both too much and too little – then they would be able to create an environment where employees wanted to expend more effort because there would be greater benefits and interest for them in doing so. Let us make this clear – this is not about wringing out more effort, extorting more work; it is about gaining discretionary effort. This involves people contributing at the best of their ability because they are *able* to – there are no barriers to their making a contribution, no hurdles they need to expend valuable effort climbing over; and because they *want* to – they find the experience fulfilling. In other words, discretionary effort can be described as what is possible – what the employee can give over and above what is targeted and paid for.

To understand why this is the case we have to return to two of the basic maxims laid out in the earlier chapters of this book. The first of these is that stress should not be synonymous with overwork. Being stressed does not necessarily mean being overburdened. Stress occurs when pressures combine in such a way that they outstrip individual capacity to cope. Lack of recognition, the pressures of managing home and work, or coping with too many daily hassles are as much a source of pressure for some people as work overload might be to others. The effects these different pressures have on job and organisational satisfaction are frequently indistinguishable from each other. Second, most employees are willing to exchange their time for money but they require something more – some form of fulfilment for them personally.

Keeping these two points in mind we can see that stress undermines our ability to release discretionary effort from our employees. It makes sense to recognise that if you can remove the barriers to peak performance then you can expect increased performance. Conversely employees can battle for only so long against issues that frustrate and demotivate them before they start to care less and contribute less. The unrecognised, unsupported and unfulfilled employee will not go the extra mile. Not because they don't want to necessarily but because they can see no point – as an employee once said, 'I do 80 an hour. I could do a 100 but I can't be bothered.' In this case this was not an attitude problem but a morale problem – there seemed no point because the effort he put into achieving 80 an hour was not recognised or appreciated. Why bother to contribute another 25% if no one is going to notice? On the other hand there are the employees who feel they want to contribute more – but they are simply unable to. So much effort is expended just staying afloat that the employee has no more to give. The loss from the organisation's point of view is that a lot of this effort is wasted and non-productive; employees who are battling with a lack of support, a lack of recognition, or poor working relationships are wasting effort and becoming stressed. How much value would there be for your organisation in removing some of those barriers to performance and refocusing that effort directly back into profit-making activities?

Making a difference

Understanding that stress can adversely affect everyone's performance, not just the few people who may be at risk from a breakdown, makes businesses more willing to look at the issue of stress at work and invest in interventions that will help everyone instead of providing remedial help for the few. It is imperative that those who need urgent help get it, of course, but there are clear benefits for the

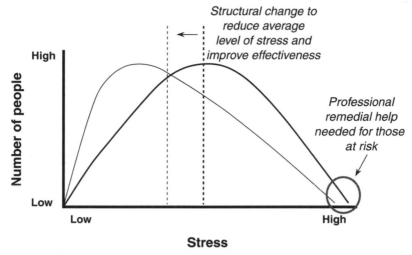

Figure 4.4 *Shifting the mean*

organisation in taking steps to reduce each employee's personal level of stress. As we have already seen, doing so can mean incremental productivity improvement across the whole workforce.

Figure 4.4 serves to illustrate that there is a clear payback in shifting the mean level of stress back towards the Y-axis. The distance between the two broken vertical lines created as a result of reducing the average overall level of stress represents the productivity, creativity and profitability improvement of reducing the average level of stress in the organisation. Or put another way, it represents the potential for discretionary effort.

FIVE

Quantifying the Stress Problem

In these early chapters we have explored the nature of employee stress and some of the ways in which stress can manifest itself at an organisational level. We have looked at how we can measure the cost, and at how we can tell if stress may be a problem. But how can we quantify it more precisely? How can we measure how widespread it is? How do we know how many people are affected, and how badly? And, perhaps most importantly, how can we find out what is causing it?

The good news is that in our experience you can find answers to these questions. This and the following chapters shift the focus to examine how you might go about quantifying and then proactively managing stress within your department or your organisation. First, some basic rules that should underpin your approach.

The need for a structured approach

Making progress with stress requires the organisation to adopt a structured approach. Tackling any large issue requires us to have a plan, and stress is no exception. Approaching the issues in a haphazard way, or starting at the treatment end rarely makes much of a lasting difference. The initiatives that work the best are those where a structured investigation and careful interpretation of findings precede any intervention. We describe this process as the investigate–interpret–intervene model (see Figure 5.1).

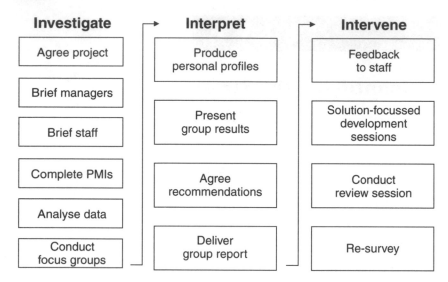

Figure 5.1 *Process overview (investigate – interpret – intervene)*

Know the problem

The starting point for managing stress in your workplace is to begin with a well-structured investigation in order to give a clear under-standing of the size and nature of the problems you are seeking to address. This may sound obvious, but the vast proportion of stress management initiatives fail because this basic principle has been overlooked. Well-meaning managers rush into treatment before they've done the diagnostics. They spend the money and resources fixing the wrong things for the wrong people at the wrong time. Initiatives are implemented with the best of intentions but they often end up as no more than a proliferation of non-integrated interven-tions addressing the wrong problem with the wrong work groups. This is usually because there was insufficient investment in investiga-tion at the outset. It is essential to have a thorough understanding of the real issues you face before you move into intervention. Managing stress is subject to the same basic principles as the management of physical health complaints; the more accurate the diagnosis, the greater the chance of identifying the most effective course of treatment. Conversely you are unlikely to make progress addressing the outcomes if you have no understanding of what is causing the problem in the first place.

A formal investigation should therefore precede any attempts at intervention. But what are we looking for?

What to measure – personal issues

Organisational stress does not exist in the equipment, plant and the machinery. If a fire alarm sounds and people evacuate the building, all the stress and pressure moves to the car park. Stress resides in the people. It therefore follows that you cannot measure organisational stress without getting into the level of individual detail. Investigation at this stage is really about asking the people how they feel. What issues and concerns do they have? What would they change if they could? You cannot get at the information any other way.

There are a number of ways that you can do this, but they all distil down into one of two approaches: you can ask them face-to-face or you can get their feedback via a questionnaire. Both have their merits and are most beneficial when used in combination with each other. In this and the next chapter we will look closely at each of them. The point is that you cannot build an organisational 'view from the bridge' without getting individual employees involved. If you were hoping to be able to measure stress and act on the results more covertly, then we are sorry to be the bearers of bad news. It is not possible. The observable effects such as absence, attrition and accidents will tell you if you have a problem, but they can't tell you what is causing it. The stress reaction is too personal and the individual perception of pressure too variable to be able to make assumptions about the nature and extent of the problem. You have to get the employees involved. Each one of them asked to participate in the investigative phase will give you a 'micro' picture of stress in your workplace. The 'macro' picture emerges when those responses are combined and interpreted in a way that tells you about the groups that are most at risk and where the most common sources of pressure lie.

Identify the hazards

The Health and Safety Executive (HSE) has produced a reference guide to tackling work-related stress, which applies a formal risk assessment process to the problem. The guide lists seven major risk factors as described below.

1. *Culture* – of the organisation and how it approaches work-related stress;
2. *Demands* – such as workload and exposure to physical hazards;
3. *Control* – how much say the person has in the way they do their work;
4. *Relationships* – covering issues such as bullying and harassment;
5. *Change* – how organisational change is managed and communicated in the organisation;
6. *Role* – whether the individual understands their role in the organisation; and whether the organisation ensures that the person does not have conflicting roles;
7. *Support, training and factors* unique to the individual:
   - *support* – from peers and line management;
   - *training* – for the person to be able to undertake the core functions of the job;
   - *factors* unique to the individual – catering for individual differences

Table 5.1 From *Guide to Tackling Work Related Stress – A Managers' Guide to Improving and Maintaining Employee Health and Well-being*. Crown copyright 2001. Reproduced by permission of the HSE.

In addition to understanding the nature of the pressures on your staff, you also need to be able to evaluate the *effects* of those pressures on your staff. Exposure to pressure is not the same as exposure to physical or environmental hazards. As we have already seen, it's the individual interpretation of that pressure that determines whether or not it is a hazard to that particular individual. After all, one person's job autonomy is another's role ambiguity! In the physical world each individual may have a different level of tolerance for noise, vibration, chemical exposure, etc. but all of these are to some extent harmful to the individual employee. This is simply not the case with psychosocial pressures. To take an extreme example, there is no possibility that one of your people will thrive when exposed to asbestos; however, it is highly likely that at least one of your employees will be positively stimulated by a challenging workload.

The task, therefore, is to find out not only what the pressures are but also the extent to which they harm your employees. Take the example of an organisation where staff are reporting pressure from the workload. The organisation would respond in a completely different way depending on whether the employees reported high levels of mental and physical health and high job satisfaction or reported poor mental and physical health and low job satisfaction.

This integrated approach to measuring both the inputs – the hazards or risk factors – and the outputs – the effect of pressure – underlines the structure of the Pressure Management Indicator (PMI). This questionnaire reports on the dynamics of the stress process described in the section on the four-way model of stress and assesses these factors in term of Effects, Sources and Individual Differences in the following measurement scales:

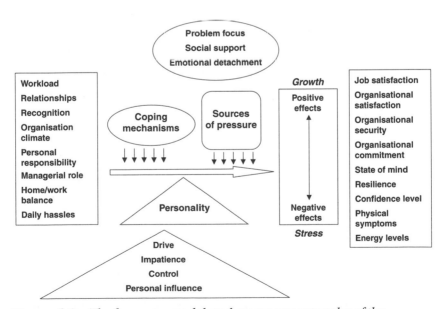

Figure 5.2 *The four-way model and measurement scales of the Pressure Management Indicator*
Copyright © 1999 Resource Systems, Harrogate, UK. Used with permission.

Talking to people

So, faced with the plethora of hazards and individual responses, how do we start to quantify the stress problem? Trying to guess the way each of your employees will react to the multitude of pressures facing them at home and at work is fraught with difficulty. There is so much that is unknown and so many variables to consider that even the most caring manager may be tempted to give up and move on to an easier issue. Talking to staff about their problems, fears and concerns is an obvious place to start an investigation; the only problem with this approach is that in many workplaces it can be extremely stressful for both interviewer and interviewee!

When we look at stress in organisations, it's quite easy to talk to managers and tell them they should talk about the pressure their people are under and listen to their answers. The problem is that many managers find that very uncomfortable. In one of our favourite Dilbert cartoons, Dilbert's boss describes the situation that managers fear more than anything else in the world: the knock on the door followed by that awful question, 'Do you have a minute?' Managers know that when an employee says, 'excuse me, do you have a minute?' that it's the 'touchy-feely stuff'. It's not nice easy problems about production schedules or finances; it's the hard part of managing, the bit where the employee might get emotional, the time when managers feel most uncomfortable and out of their depth. But hearing how people experience pressure in the business and the way that it affects them is a necessary part of moving forward with the issues.

If discussions with your staff about how they feel and how they're coping are an everyday event, handled in confidence and mutual trust, then this is an excellent way to gain an understanding of the issues. People will talk to you openly and honestly about their problems, will tell you without being asked that they're struggling or are under-stimulated. They will trust you to see if you can remedy the problems without evoking fear of retribution or their being thought weak or 'emotional'. Unfortunately, in most organisations, these sorts of conversations are extremely rare indeed. It is far more usual to find that staff find it difficult to share their feelings with management and would regard questions about their 'stress' as inappropriate and intrusive.

Unless you're one of the fortunate managers who has the type of open and honest dialogue we've just described – in which case you probably don't have a big stress problem anyway – then you have to approach the topic with care. There is a very real danger of making things worse instead of better, as stress levels increase because people are worried about what's going on and are suspicious of your motives. 'Why am I being asked these questions? Do they think I can't cope? Are they thinking of getting rid of me?' are reasonable responses to a sudden surge of interest in employee welfare.

There is also the problem of how stress-inducing this process can be for the manager herself. Some managers find it enormously difficult to adopt the right tone, or even to accept that this is a legitimate part of their job. For these people the idea of having to have a 'personal' discussion with one of their employees, especially about something as sensitive as stress, fills them with dread. Under these circumstances the conversation is unlikely to go well.

An alternative approach is to talk to your employees in a group and get them to share their concerns. However, as with the one-to-one interviews, the context has to be right. If these sorts of group discussions are an unusual event in your organisation then talking about stress is not a good place to start!

We had a good example of the problems of trying to initiate open discussion in a culture that doesn't expect or support these initiatives. We worked with one, highly autocratic organisation whose regional manager was worried about the stress of his employees. He was a very kind, caring individual but had a very formal command and control management style. He asked us to help after he'd spent three embarrassing months trying to get his staff to say something in his weekly 'get it off your chest' meetings. In these meetings he got all of his 100 employees in the canteen and asked them to tell him what was on their mind in an 'open and honest way'. He had his secretary there to take notes and promised he would look into all the matters that they raised. He introduced the session, reminding them he was there to listen and to help and then sat down and waited for their comments. When he told us about the failure of these meetings he was completely bewildered. Except for a couple of minor complaints about the toilets and the canteen food, in all of these hour-long meetings no one had ever said anything. 'Does this mean that they don't have any problems?' he asked.

His mistake was obvious. Rather than invite 100 employees to 'bare all' in an open environment, he would have had more success if he had gone into various work areas and spent some time with his people in an informal discussion where he would have been able to explain his interest in their feedback, reassure them about how he would use the information, and build confidence. In a culture where there have been few attempts at seeking employee input, a sudden interest in people's views is likely to cause suspicion about management motives. If he had put fewer people on the spot publicly and stimulated confidential discussion on their territory, about their issues, he would have created an environment where individuals felt it was safe to speak up. It's not surprising that toilets and canteen food were the only feedback, as these are safe things to mention and give nothing away about the person brave enough to raise them. We shall say more about how to get the best from group discussion later in this chapter.

Look for sources and symptoms

In conducting an investigation into stress it is essential to look for the sources as well as the effects of stress. Being able to measure the effects is useful for building awareness and constructing the business case for action, but knowing about the sources and addressing them produces more effective and longer-lasting benefits than treating the symptoms. With a clear understanding of the source of the problems and the groups of people who are most affected, there is a much greater chance of designing appropriate, effective and lasting interventions. Group or individual discussions taking place during the investigative phase should focus equally on gathering information about *how* people feel as well as *why* they feel that way. Understanding the '*why*' will point us in the right direction to identify potential solutions. Indeed the fastest way to gain a clear picture of the real source of the problem is to ask those affected to describe where they are now and ask them to think through and tell you 'what would make a difference'. We will be looking at this approach in more detail shortly, but for now the point is that investigation is about getting a feel for both the sources and the symptoms. You need to know both.

Many companies that we have worked with were surprised to find that when they asked the questions the responses were not what they had expected. They are pleasantly surprised to find that far from major structural issues that would require complex and expensive interventions to address, the staff have much more manageable concerns.

The most common example of this is where companies expect to find that their teams are creaking under an excessive workload, only to discover that workload hardly features as an issue at all. Instead employees report pressure and stress from a lack of communication or recognition for the work that they do. The message emerging in these cases is that employees feel they could actually achieve more, if they felt more personally involved in what they were being asked to do and felt recognised for the contribution they make. This example works well to illustrate that action based on imperfect understanding can be an expensive waste of resources, whilst also leaving the underlying problem unaddressed. In this case an unpopular (and probably fruitless!) request to the financial director for a 10% uplift in headcount to address the work overload would have produced no impact at all. Except of course that it would have added considerably to the cost base of the department, and in this example, to increased anxiety about job security. The appropriate intervention in this case was simpler and much less costly to implement than any of the preconceived ideas the company had prior to the survey. They simply had to find ways of letting the staff know that their work was appreciated.

A step-by-step guide to identifying the problem

To guide you through the process of a structured assessment of workplace stress we advocate a two-stage approach.

1. The first stage is designed to help you see the progress you can make using your own resources and expertise. It will help you gain an insight into the issues facing your staff and should give some idea of the scale of the problem as well as some of the sources. The focus here is on making use of the information on your doorstep, but help from your colleagues and internal or external facilitators may be valuable and provide additional information.
2. The second stage provides much more detailed and reliable information and uses a well-proven, structured method for investigating the nature and extent of stress through a combination of questionnaires and focus groups. This is described in the next chapter.

Stage one

Planning

There is an old saying – 'fail to prepare, prepare to fail'. Given the sensitivities that surround stress, this maxim is particularly worth remembering. Before you ask a single question, think through what it is that you want to know, who you need to ask, who you have to tell, and who you need to involve. If it helps, write down three questions that you most want the answers to. For example, do we have a problem? Who might be affected? What are the major sources? Make sure from that point on that you structure each activity to provide answers to at least these questions and stay close to the investigate–interpret–intervene model. In other words, place most emphasis in your planning on how you will 'find out' – don't worry too much about second-guessing what you will do when you have the information. That will become clearer once you have collected feedback and interpreted what you found. Then you need to think about the resources you have around you that can help and become involved.

Stakeholder analysis

'Stakeholder analysis' is a grand term for thinking through 'who do I need to get involved?' Plenty of people beside those directly involved or affected will have an opinion, but who can add value to the process? As has already been said, conducting an investigation means that you are going to have to get employees involved – there is a limit to the amount you can find out by other means.

It is clear that getting groups of employees involved means that their managers are going to have to be part of the process too. In choosing who to involve, the primary consideration is to involve the staff that are most likely to be able to give you the information that you need. If, however, you can involve teams whose managers are supportive and do not feel threatened by the process then so much the better. This is not just because your enquiries will be more fruitful. We should also remember that this is the first part of a structured approach that eventually leads to an intervention phase. This means that people are going to have to do some things differently. It is important, therefore, to build a network of managers right from the start, who have a genuine interest in the outcome and who want to act on the information you produce.

Supportive line managers are a critical group for you to work with, but you need to think through who else might need to become involved. What about HR? What about trade unions and staff representatives? What about occupational health? Work out who you will need to communicate with before you get a phone call from them asking why they were not consulted and involved! Go back to your original research objectives and ask yourself two questions: 'What do I want to know?' and 'Who needs to be involved because they might have insights to share or data that I can use?' Once you get going you will be amazed how many resources are at your disposal and how much information you already have!

Last, and most important, think through who already has responsibility for stress and for making things better. Technically the answer
to that is of course 'everybody who works here', but in practice this is
a responsibility not everybody is aware of. Who does have an interest
in stress and already has this on their agenda? Who perhaps should
have the greatest interest by having the most to lose if we get this
wrong? Get these people involved in your plans and get them
contributing from the beginning – it will pay dividends!

Desk research

To supplement the information you will gain by talking to staff and
managers you should also review the data that you know already
exists. You might for example want to ask your OH advisors
how many people they have seen who are suffering from stress.
Without asking them to break individual confidentiality, ask for
their insights into the primary effects and sources of stress in the
cases they have seen. Do they appear to be primarily a result of
work-related issues, home-related issues or home–work balance
issues?

Similarly review the absence data that you have. What is the level
of self-reported stress-related ill health? What proportion of frequent
short-term absences do you feel could be stress-related? If you can
interrogate the data in this way, can you see whether some
departments, work groups or job types are more affected by frequent
short-term absence than others? What might this mean?

Look at attrition data. What is your rate of turnover? What are
people saying at exit interview? How many of the reasons they are
giving for leaving might have a stress component? What about
productivity figures? Can you see any measured or observable effects
on productivity, profitability, efficiency, creativity, and customer
service? In your view does there seem to be a relationship between
stress and absence, accidents or staff turnover? What would you
estimate it might be costing your organisation overall?

Take time to collect and think about the information you already
have – the quantitative information available to you. Then start to

collect the qualitative data from the people. The quantitative data will give you insights into how to structure your qualitative investigation. If you do it this way round you will have a much greater chance of asking the right questions.

Group discussions

We talked earlier in the chapter about the merits and demerits of talking to people one to one or in a group. Both approaches have their benefits and a good investigation will probably make use of both. In our experience though it is the discussion group format that yields the biggest benefits. This seems to be for a variety of reasons. Amongst them is that a group of about 10 people is small enough to feel confidential and non-threatening and large enough to stimulate debate and cross-fertilisation of ideas between participants. People worry about facilitating focus groups but, in our experience – providing you've done the preparation and people know why they're there and the rules of engagement – they are surprisingly easy. Often all you need to do is ask a few open questions and the group will do the rest for you!

Here are a few pointers to remember to get the best results from a group discussion.

Pre-communication

When selecting the groups of people you want to talk to, remember to explain what the meeting is about, why you are interested in their input, what they will be required to do and what you will do with the information. It is also worth letting them know who else is being invited so they can see for themselves that there is a good spread of people and they have not been picked for any sinister reason. These early messages are essential if you are to draw in willing participants who are comfortable in giving you the information you need. It is no good getting people to attend against their will, or trying to work with a group of people who are so suspicious of the sudden interest in their welfare that they assume the worst and stay mute throughout!

Setting the scene

At the start of the meeting take time to allow people to settle and relax. Set the scene, remind and reassure once again why you need their help and what you are going to do with the information.

Open questions

Paying attention to how you ask a question is an important discipline and dramatically affects the answers you get back. Wherever possible, ask questions in a way that encourages more than a yes-or-no answer. If you can encourage people to talk freely then you need to ask a lot fewer questions to get the information you need. People will also feel less threatened and enjoy what will feel like a discussion rather than an interrogation. This feeling produces a virtuous circle of greater confidence in the process and therefore more open information-giving. The rhyme 'I had seven friends who taught me all l knew: I called them what, when, where, which, how, why and who!' is the most useful way to remember how to ask what are known as 'open questions'. The same technique works very well when we are dealing with what might be a sensitive area. Ask only open questions and listen carefully to the answers. Remember we are trying to understand how people feel and where they believe the sources of the problems to be. You do not have to agree with them, and in any event your opinion is irrelevant to the discussion. Listen and take notes if necessary, being careful to note the group consensus and particular concerns rather than obvious 'soapbox' issues. Some questions you might like to ask are:

- How is pressure felt in the business?
- What effect does it have on morale/satisfaction with the job/ satisfaction with the organisation?
- What other effects are there?
- What do the group feel are the major sources of pressure?
- Why are these a problem?
- How does that make them feel?
- How do they deal with these feelings?
- Where do they go if they have a stress problem? What do they do about it?

- What issues do they have with the way work/their role is organised?
- Are these issues better or worse amongst particular groups of employees?
- If so, what accounts for the difference?
- What correlations might there be with grade, location, job type, age, gender, length of service?
- What little things get in the way of getting the job done?

Moving towards solutions

The golden rule in using group discussion to gather qualitative information about stress is to keep the discussion focused on the sources and the effects and to constantly invite participants to volunteer their view of what would make a difference. The meeting should not be allowed to degenerate into a free-for-all moan!

The sessions need to be positioned and remembered in a positive way. Therefore whilst participants need to be given time to air their views – you have after all asked them to the meeting specifically to do that – you need to ask at regular intervals for input to "What would make a difference?" This will not only prevent the meeting from shifting into a negative gear but will also give clear pointers about possible interventions. Management teams who make assumptions about what people's issues are usually also commit the same error when they decide what will make a difference. If you ask the people with the problems they will invariably come up with a solution that is smaller and more easily implemented than anything you could have thought up on your own. You have to be at the coalface to know what tool does the job best. So – ask them what, given the chance, they would do about it.

Some other questions you could ask to start moving towards solutions:

- What interventions do they think might have the most rapid and beneficial effect in improving the way people feel?
- What interventions do they think might have the most rapid and beneficial effect in reducing the pressures they have identified at source?

- What would they change?
- If they came into work the next morning and things were better, what would they notice that was different?

It is also worth exploring what people like. What works well now? What should we do more of? These are particularly good questions to ask towards the end of the session so the last words said were focused on the positive rather than the negative.

Where are we now?

When you have conducted your discussion groups, collated your information and interpreted the results in the light of your 'desk research', you will have sufficient information to form a judgement about the extent to which your organisation has a problem. Being able to answer the 'Where are we now?' question is a vital part of the process and one that dictates the direction of your intervention. We will be looking at this more closely in Chapter 9.

Remember – this isn't about pure research, it's about making a difference. The act of observation, especially when it's done through involvement and questioning, starts to change what is being observed. This is particularly noticeable in focus groups where the beneficial effect of simply asking people to talk about their issues produces a positive change in their attitude. We notice time and time again people arriving for the focus group discussions tired, dejected and fed-up, and leaving full of energy and enthusiasm. Unfortunately, in the absence of meaningful change in the workplace, this improvement in morale soon wears off. Focus groups are an important element in the process, but they will not, in themselves, change anything.

What if this isn't enough?

The approaches we've just described will make a significant difference to your level of understanding and should, from the very beginning of the process, start to rectify some of the problems. At the very least you are showing your people that you care about them, value their wellbeing and their opinions and are involving them in finding workable solutions. In many workplaces that, in itself, will go a long way to reducing stress. However, sometimes the informal approach isn't enough. The problems are too big, too widespread or too difficult to get to without more sophisticated tools. The following chapter describes how to drill below the surface to get a much deeper and more comprehensive understanding.

SIX

Gaining a Deeper Understanding – Stress Surveys

Just talking to people will tell you a good deal of what you need to know about whether stress issues exist in your workplace. One of the shortcomings of using this approach as the only method of information gathering is that the 'evidence' is highly subjective and easily influenced by the way in which the questions were asked and how the session is conducted. As many a manager who has been down this route will tell you, there will be plenty of people in the organisation who will take the information that you show them and find ways of undermining its accuracy or completeness; 'They would say that wouldn't they' being the favourite way of dismissing the evidence as inadmissible. You may therefore need to supplement your investigation with more objective measurement tools.

The need for hard facts

In most organisations it's a lot easier to get things done if you can quantify the problem with objective evidence. Saying that '5% of our workforce are reporting mental ill health at or above levels of psychiatric out-patients and 65% of those have work-related issues that give them a strong case for a workers' compensation claim that could cost the company over £200 000 each' is much more powerful than saying, 'I think we've got a stress problem.' Collecting evidence through a reliable and valid survey process provides high quality data that the manager, HR director or chief medical officer can present to the board or senior management team as a rational, well-analysed business case.

When you can present objective data about the issues, stress ceases to be a 'soft' welfare issue – difficult to quantify and therefore easy to ignore. With the right tools you can collect hard evidence, supported by good benchmarking data, which can be used to make decisions. The outcome of a properly conducted stress audit will be a sound business case that can be discussed in the same way as any other investment or resourcing decision.

Questionnaires

The most commonly accepted way of obtaining 'hard' evidence about the nature and extent of occupational stress is to ask your employees to complete a questionnaire designed to quantify the issues you wish to measure. There are two distinct approaches to deciding what sort of questionnaire you wish to use. Either you can write your own questions, producing an in-house instrument; or you can use a commercially available, standardised questionnaire. Whichever approach you take you should make sure that the questionnaire does what it's meant to do before releasing it on your workforce! Table 6.1 shows the design characteristics of a stress questionnaire. Table 6.2 shows the measurement domains of the PMI as an example of what a stress questionnaire should measure.

To produce an instrument that would provide an integrated, comprehensive, relevant, compact, and accurate measure of occupational stress, the questionnaire should:

- be quick to complete and non-threatening;
- have high levels of validity and reliability;
- achieve an optimum level of utility and power;
- be able to be used by everyone in the organisation;
- be used in different occupational settings;
- work across cultural boundaries; and
- identify organisation-specific issues and reflect the changing demands on people at work.

Table 6.1 *Design characteristics of a stress questionnaire*

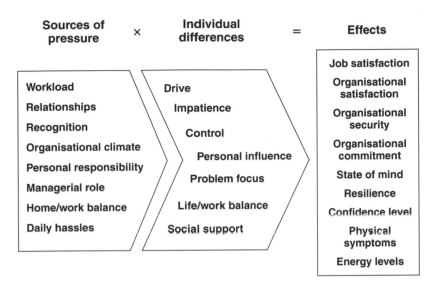

Table 6.2 *Potential measurement domains of the PMI*

Psychometric properties

A detailed discussion of psychometrics or the minutiae of question-naire design is outside the scope of this book. However, it is important to touch on some of the key criteria for judging the technical quality of a questionnaire. The first step is to make sure that the underlying assumptions governing the design of the question-naire are explicit and are consistent with what you are trying to achieve. For a standardised instrument you will need to know the underlying model on which it is based and the theoretical framework that supports this model. For an in-house questionnaire make sure you are clear about your assumptions and that they are supported by empirical evidence.

Following on from this you need to consider the comprehen-siveness of the questionnaire. Is it going to measure all the variables that you consider relevant to understanding workplace stress? One of the biggest weaknesses of a number of stress questionnaires is that they measure only a small part of the stress process. For example, some standardised questionnaires, developed from clinical mental health measures, look only at the effects of stress; they provide no information about what's causing stress. A common failing of in-house questionnaires is that they measure only sources of pressure. They may tell the organisation that workload is high but provide no information about whether the staff experience this as good (stimulated) or bad (overworked). There is clearly a trade-off between the comprehensiveness of a questionnaire and its conciseness, and we'll examine this in more detail in the section on length of questionnaires.

The two key psychometric properties that need to be assessed are validity and reliability. In order to provide useful information, a questionnaire needs to be both valid and reliable. In other words it needs to measure what it purports to measure and it needs to do it with as little error as possible. Demonstrating the validity of a questionnaire can be a long and difficult process and, without extensive, time-consuming research, can be very hard to do for an in-house instrument. If you are designing your own questionnaire then beware of face validity. Just because a particular question looks as if it's asking about a specific construct doesn't necessarily mean that it is. With a standardised questionnaire the publishers should be able to provide detailed validity studies and quote values for different measures of validity such as predictive validity, construct validity, or discriminant validity. The second key psychometric property is that the questionnaire should be reliable. Reliability is the consistency of measurement; it shows the relationship between a questionnaire's ability to measure the underlying construct as opposed to measurement error. High reliability means that the questionnaire, or scale, is measuring signal, not noise!

With a standardised instrument the test publisher should be able to refer you to papers in peer-reviewed journals describing the psychometric properties of their questionnaire. For in-house questionnaires the situation is much more difficult. In practice few organisations seem to carry out any formal evaluation of the questionnaires they design themselves and may easily end up distributing thousands of questionnaires that simply don't measure what the survey organisers think they are measuring. It's as if the company decided to measure stock movement by counting the number of shoppers visiting their stores or measure cash flow by counting the number rather than the value of the cheques they issue and receive. The computer industry talks about 'garbage in, garbage out'; this is true of stress surveys. Don't expect to get meaningful results from a bad questionnaire!

Length of questionnaires

An important consideration in choosing a stress survey instrument is the length of time it takes people to complete it. A short questionnaire is obviously quick to fill in but may leave participants feeling that the survey has not covered the issues that matter or are relevant to them. Too many questions and the effort involved in participating will cause people to lose interest and answer questions inaccurately. In our experience the optimum time for co-operative participation is around 15 to 20 minutes. Because of the amount of time involved in getting people to participate in the process and the time taken to physically administer the questionnaire, a shorter instrument adds little benefit – if it takes five minutes to get ready to do the questionnaire, and five minutes to collect replies and get back to work, there seems little point in only taking five minutes to complete the questionnaire! However, if it takes more than 20 minutes to complete you start to get two problems. Concentration wavers, people become tired, feel it's too much effort and the quality of responses to later questions will be worse than for questions at the beginning.

The second factor is being away from work. Most employers can spare people for 30 minutes, but 45 or 60 minutes is more difficult. This last point is important because although employees might choose to complete the questionnaire in their own time, the offer should always be made to participate during work time. This signals that this is a legitimate work activity and sends the right positive message about the priority that is being given to capturing individual opinions. The issue of completing questionnaires in work or personal time is important and we deal with it more fully later in this chapter.

Relevance and completeness

Another vital consideration is the relevance and completeness of the questionnaire. What is it measuring? Is it looking for specific issues or generic ones? How close are the measurement domains to the real issues that you are trying to uncover? What use will you be able to put the final results to? How will the data be used in practical terms? It is self-evident that you must be able to see a good fit between the questions asked and your objectives. Far too many stress surveys are conducted only to produce a mountain of data that is interesting but incomplete or of limited use because the most relevant areas were missed completely.

By definition standardised questionnaires need to be exactly that. They need to ask a fixed number of questions on the generic issues that have been proven to be a factor in the stress process. As has been said already this has many benefits, not the least being the ability to benchmark and draw meaningful conclusions about how your organisation's pressure profile compares with others. It does mean, however, that it is difficult to capture the nuances and unique local issues that are a feature of each workplace. As a minimum, your questionnaire should cover the key risk factors undertaken in the HSE 'Guide to Tackling Work Related Stress' as described on p. 56.

Developing an organisation-specific questionnaire

Testing for specific issues

We've explored the strengths and weaknesses of standardised and in-house questionnaires and found that both have their advantages and disadvantages. One way of achieving the best of both worlds is to use a standardised instrument and supplement it with your own organisation-specific questions. These additional items can be added to ensure that issues not measured by the core instrument are monitored (see Table 6.3). For example, issues such as harassment in the workplace, discrimination at work, bullying, and the fairness of

Additional Questions

This section helps us to gain a better understanding of specific issues affecting wellbeing and motivation. Please indicate the extent to which you agree or disagree with the following statements. If a question does not apply to you, circle the 'Very Strongly Disagree' box.

Key Issues

	1 Very strongly disagree	2 Strongly disagree	3 Disagree	4 Agree	5 Strongly agree	6 Very strongly agree
1. Communication between managers and staff is good.	1	2	3	4	5	6
2. I find domestic arrangements difficult to plan because of my working patterns.	1	2	3	4	5	6
3. My line manager gives me a lot of support.	1	2	3	4	5	6
4. There is too much training.	1	2	3	4	5	6
5. I am kept well informed about what is going on by my immediate manager.	1	2	3	4	5	6
6. I think the level of on-going training is good.	1	2	3	4	5	6
7. I understand what I am supposed to be doing.	1	2	3	4	5	6
8. I find it hard to manage the physical demands of my job.	1	2	3	4	5	6
9. I have less influence over how I do my job than I used to	1	2	3	4	5	6
10. My working patterns are a source of pressure to me.	1	2	3	4	5	6

Table 6.3 *Sample supplementary questions*

Copyright © 2001 Resource Systems, Harrogate, UK. Used with permission.

grievance and disciplinary procedures may be relevant to an organisation's understanding of stress at work.

In one recent example a company had relocated and restructured in such a way that well-established employees were now travelling considerable distances to get to the workplace. This was considered a major source of pressure for that group and and they felt an item covering this needed to be added in order for the instrument to be relevant. As already mentioned in the discussion on relevance and completeness, before starting the survey it is important to see if there is anything else that is not measured by the core instrument that should be included. Obviously there is a compromise between length and comprehensiveness, and there is little point in having the most all-embracing questionnaire if no one has the time to complete it.

Who should we survey?

Choosing your survey population correctly is a big determinant of the success and usefulness of the whole exercise. There are few hard and fast rules about who to include but there are a few guidelines.

We have said all along that you should start with the end in mind. Why am I doing this piece of work? What do I want to find out? Most importantly, how will the information be put to use when I have it? Answers to these questions should determine the shape and dimensions of the population you involve. Broadly speaking there are two different approaches you can take.

Sampling and sample size

The instinctive response from most managers when asked about sample size is to think of surveying staff at random and in sufficient number to be able to feel that the results are statistically significant and representative of the employees as a whole. This approach has a number of drawbacks.

The first of these is that if you are a large company it means getting completed questionnaires back from a high proportion of your workforce. It is difficult to be precise about the best proportion because of the unknown level of variability in the data. If, for example, you have a very similar workforce doing similar jobs in similar situations and your initial analysis suggests that they all experience stress and pressure in roughly the same ways, then you may assume that you only need to sample a small proportion – say 20% – to get a representative picture of the workforce as a whole. If, on the other hand, you have a diverse workforce doing different jobs in different locations, you will need a much higher proportion to give you an estimate of the workforce as a whole, say 70 to 80%.

In our experience, the differences within an organisation are usually much greater than the similarities. Time and time again, we present survey results for the company with the warning 'beware of averages'. As you will see in Chapter 7, we show a graph with the overall results and then show how meaningless this is when we break the data down by department or grade or location. In most organisations, the company average is the equivalent of adding chalk to cheese. And about as useful!

If your sample size is too small, or if you don't capture departmental, location or other classification data on the questionnaires, you may end up with meaningless data that masks the useful information trapped within. In order to be sure you have the right people in the right groups to be able to analyse your data at the right level, you will inevitably have to survey a large proportion of your staff.

This turns your survey into a rather high profile activity that will probably involve you in a lot of interdepartmental discussions about process, downtime, outcomes and so on. If you are a smaller company then these issues may not be so acute but they can be show-stoppers for larger workforces.

The second problem with this approach is the way in which the resultant data can be used. If your objective is to gain an overview of the extent to which you have a stress problem then representative samples are a good route. The problems can arise when you want to move from analysis to intervention. *Stress measurement must lead to stress management*. This means that different groups are going to need to do something differently. A sample taken across the business usually makes it difficult for any one group to adopt the results and take them forward as, by definition, they were developed by amalgamating the responses gathered from all over the business.

We shall revisit this theme in Chapter 7 when we look at data analysis and again in Chapter 9 when we look at appropriate interventions. In nearly every case that we have seen, the most sustainable improvements come when specific work groups have been able to identify the issues that affect them and work with the information to develop their own 'small-step' solutions. Representative sample studies make this difficult if not impossible in larger companies. If 20 departments or business functions participated you cannot assume that one intervention will suit them all. If you break the data down into separate departmental reports then you can identify the variability between departments but you may have insufficient people in each of the areas to convince local managers that, even though the survey is statistically representative overall, their results are representative of their area as a whole.

As has already been said, the smaller company may be able to comfortably include all staff and this latter issue is therefore avoided. In this ideal case, the results are truly everybody's information and can subsequently be 'owned' and worked on by all who participated.

Work group studies

If resources mean that the number of people involved in the study is limited then a more manageable approach for the larger company is to go for a deeper understanding of a smaller section of the business or particular business function. This has the obvious benefit of limiting the number of managers who need to be involved at the 'buy-in' stage. It also encourages a deeper interest and relationship with the work by the management team than might be the case in a more global approach. As we shall see in Chapter 9, this will pay dividends when you get to the 'making a difference' stage.

A word of caution about any selection process, and this applies whatever the sampling method used. It is vitally important that you provide reassurance to those individuals or teams that are being invited, that they are not being singled out 'because we think you have a problem'. If people are left with this feeling then not only will your response rate suffer but also you will have sent a message that undermines confidence in the whole process. Be open about the criteria you have used to make your selection even if that means a public recognition that 'we know that as a department you are under a lot of pressure'. The message is that 'we want to understand where that pressure comes from and how we may be able to influence the issues' rather than 'we want to know how stressed you are'.

It is also worth thinking about including work groups who are felt to handle pressure particularly well. In other words, when you are deciding which teams to include don't always focus purely on the groups who are thought most likely to have a problem. A lot of stress management is about stress avoidance and there are models of good practice in most organisations that other departments not so well able to cope might be able to learn from. Once again this is something we will come back to in Chapter 9.

The major guideline in selection is to think through how the information will be used to make a difference. If your survey does uncover some issues, then those issues are likely only to be resolved if something is subsequently done differently. This gives you two challenges. First you need people to accept that there is a problem and second you have to get them to want to change. The key to both these challenges is specific, relevant and usable information. Keeping survey populations tight, and wherever possible involving complete teams, helps you in both endeavours. The whole team approach means that people get data that is specific and relevant. If it is both of these things they can work with it to develop their own small-step approaches, which is what builds interest and commitment to change.

SEVEN

Running a Stress Survey

Once you have developed or identified a measurement tool that meets your needs then, in theory, running a survey is just about distributing the questionnaires. Or is it? Before you mail a single questionnaire you must remind yourself that this is a sensitive subject. Sending questionnaires out that may ask people, for example, to self-report their level of satisfaction with their close relationships or boss requires careful planning. You need to look before you leap!

The following section represents a distillation of the best practice we have observed during the hundreds of surveys that we have conducted, involving several hundred thousand participants from companies large and small. This experience has been gained from working closely with a wide range of private and public sector employees both in the UK and throughout the world.

The questionnaire is only part of the process

The key to a successful audit is to recognise that the questionnaire is only part of the process. It is highly likely that if a stress questionnaire is sent out without the right amount of pre-planning and pre-communication the results will be disappointing. We have learnt the critical role of careful preparation the hard way. When we first started measuring stress at work we would go to organisations and say, 'We've got this questionnaire that will do a wonderful job of measuring stress at work.' We would then leave the organisation to decide how to implement the audit process and return to analyse the results. Perhaps the most important lesson we've learnt over the years is that there is more to it than that! You need a good measurement tool, of course, but on its own it is not sufficient to make the process a success. It is the whole of the audit cycle that makes the difference. The raising awareness, briefing staff on what is going to happen, getting management and trade union support, running discussion groups after the event, linking of personnel data and survey data and so on. All of these separate but related activities create an integrated approach where the whole is greater than the sum of the parts.

Effective stress measurement therefore requires forethought and project management if the results are to be useful and the employee response favourable. The principles are simple, but they need to be considered and implemented carefully.

Stakeholder analysis

In Chapter 5 we spoke about the necessity of thinking through who to get involved in any internal enquiries about the level of stress. If your formal stress audit has not been preceded by any informal research, then the process we described earlier needs to be carried out for this piece of work.

If stakeholders have already been identified then you should review the list again and check that the same people need to be briefed and involved this time. One of the benefits of stress question-naires over more informal research methods is that you can involve larger numbers of employees more quickly and more cost-effectively. As a result, there are likely to be more line managers who need to be aware and supportive of the aims and objectives of the audit.

Manager pre-communication

It is essential that you gain the support of the line managers who have responsibility for staff involved in the survey. This is for a very good reason. As we have already said, the purpose of a survey is not measurement for measurement's sake, it is about being able to act and make a difference. When the data collection process is over, and the analysis complete, somebody is going to have to do something differently. If managers were coerced into letting their people participate or were unaware of the benefits of the process and the way the information will be used, then you can guarantee that they will have no commitment to acting on the results.

It is therefore essential that line management of the teams to be involved meet and establish a common understanding. They should understand why the survey is being conducted, the survey objectives, what the outputs will be, what will happen next and their role in all of the above. Most importantly they need to have commitment to the results and be willing to adopt their team or work group output and work with the employees on it.

It goes almost without saying that line managers should also be involved in the audit itself by completing a questionnaire. One of the most predictable parts of survey work is that the pressure profiles of a group will be markedly different from the profiles of their staff. One of the regular outcomes from this work is that managers will be able to review the results and observe this difference for themselves. In many of the groups that we have worked with, this little piece of management development has, on its own, acted as an agent for improvement in the relationships between manager and team members!

However, involvement should not be confused with buy-in. Getting a senior employee to complete a stress questionnaire does not of itself signal any commitment to either the existence of a problem in their department or a willingness to act differently if required. In order to gain their full involvement it is worth remembering that at the point when they are asked to get involved they will not have your knowledge or enthusiasm for the subject. Many will feel defensive and wonder why they and their team are being approached in this way. It is also important to listen to any concerns that they may have about the process, and incorporate their observations into the project plan.

Many of the obstacles to buy-in can be removed by improving managers' understanding of the issue itself. As we have already discussed, stress is a confusing and imprecise term. When we get 15 managers in a room to discuss a stress audit we often find at least as many opinions about exactly what it is we are trying to measure! In our work with companies some time is usually spent with either individual managers or groups of managers developing their understanding of the relationship between pressure and the stress process. This helps increase both awareness and appreciation that the issue is a real one as well as build commitment towards more precise measurement. When managers are given information about stress and how it can affect people they are able to appreciate that whilst they may not be under stress right now, it may be a very real issue for some of their team members. Most importantly there usually follows a greater understanding that stress is not a sign of personal weakness after all but a process over which they have considerable influence.

Employee communication

Once the management team are aware of the scope and objectives of the project, and have agreed their roles and responsibilities towards the process, then it is time to go public. This does not, however, mean sending out a batch of questionnaires with compliment slips. If stress questionnaires arrive on employee desks without a well-thought-out communication plan then the response rates are likely to be extremely low. Worse than that, employees who are uncertain as to why they or their team have been chosen to participate are more likely to feel threatened and anxious than involved and enthused. Getting pre-communication messages right is therefore another very important part of the process. Groups of employees abhor a vacuum. If you do not explain the positive objectives and benefits of the survey, then the gap will be filled with fear and uncertainty. Don't assume your employees know your intentions are honourable! There is sadly a lot more mistrust of management motives than most managers themselves imagine.

The medium for the message

Choosing a medium for your message is probably a culturally led decision. In our experience, face-to-face briefings for groups of participants, whilst undoubtedly time-consuming, deliver the multiple benefits of being able to inform directly, answer specific questions and, by dint of the time being given away from the task, send positive messages about the importance of this work. There is also the added benefit that whilst you have groups of employees in the room, fully enthused by the benefits of the survey, you can get them to fill it in there and then! If you can get them to a briefing then you have got their input.

This approach simply does not work for some companies – particularly larger workforces with multiple locations or field-based staff, or if you have chosen to go for random sampling. E-mail is one solution for spreading messages rapidly, but of course sending e-mail is no guarantee that people will read what they get! In practice companies seem to use a variety of methods to get the messages across. The important thing is to choose the medium that means the greatest number of people will get to hear about the rationale and the process for the survey in advance of a questionnaire landing on their desk.

Confidentiality

The survey process must be confidential to the individual, and part of the message you give will be to reassure staff about this. Employees will have understandable concerns about the nature of the questions they are going to be asked and where the information they give will go. They will want to know that their managers will not see their individual responses and that they cannot be identified through the group results. Left unanswered, these worries will lead many employees to ignore the offer to participate. A good response to your survey means a larger data set, which in turn facilitates more detailed analysis and more usable management information. The message is: do as much as you can to allay fears and present the work in a positive light. In our experience it is almost impossible to overdo the amount of reassurances you can give about confidentiality. It is well worth devoting a lot of time to the security and confidentiality guarantees that you must have built into the audit process.

Protecting confidentiality is obviously easier if external consultants are involved. If the survey is being conducted in-house then a 'trusted' department such as occupational health or the counselling team should be approached to administer it.

If, despite all the assurances, people are still reluctant to complete a questionnaire then ask them to send one in anyway – even if it's blank. The objective is to encourage people to do something so that they don't sit on the sidelines because they can't be bothered. Although the surveys are voluntary it's always a good idea to make it easier for people to take part in the audit than to ignore it.

Pressure instead of stress – the need for appropriate positioning

In the early chapters we talked about pressure as an input to the stress process. Pressure is neutral, neither good nor bad. Some of the time pressures combine to produce an outcome that we know as 'stress'. At other times, or in other people, those same pressures could produce the completely different outcome of growth. It follows then that although we have been talking of 'stress surveys' and 'stress audits' we might want to be more careful in the language we use when we communicate with our employees.

When we developed the Pressure Management Indicator (PMI) – one of the most widely used instruments for measuring occupational stress – from the Occupational Stress Indicator (OSI), we changed the name to emphasise pressure and not stress for several reasons. The first is that 'stress' is a loaded and often unacceptable term in many organisations. Although it was becoming more accepted in the late 1980s and early 1990s, it was still associated with failure and weakness. People are understandably less interested in working with an instrument whose primary function, as they will see it, is to expose their own personal failures and weaknesses.

The second reason is that you find what people think you're looking for. Giving out a stress questionnaire presupposes a stress problem. If you give someone a 'stress' questionnaire they may fill it in with a stress mindset and overemphasise the negatives. Having a neutral or a positive name for the questionnaire or the intervention project is much more acceptable. In any event you are interested in how people manage pressure. As we said in early chapters, there is much more to be gained through a proactive approach to stress management than identifying the extent of your casualties.

The language we use when we introduce this work to employees is then very important. The word 'stress' is becoming more widely accepted in the workplace but that does not mean it has lost its negative associations. Many people will have built their careers in an environment where 'stress is for wimps', or have learnt to wear their stress as a badge of commitment. Any audit that sets out to involve people without thinking it through from the employee perspective will be less effective than it could have been. Talking about pressure, and labelling the work as 'pressure management' appears to us to produce the most favourable reaction. The work can then be positioned as a drive by the business to understand more about the *pressure profile* of the organisation. This approach does not presume that all who are under pressure are necessarily experiencing stress, and as a result feels less threatening. It also explains why everyone should take part in the audit. The process is relevant to everyone, not just those suffering from stress.

Increasing awareness

As has been said already there is more to a stress audit than the questionnaire. An important part of the exercise is increasing awareness and knowledge about the issues. In the same way that securing management commitment requires us to enlarge their understanding, employees also need to raise their awareness. They will have as many misconceptions about what stress is and is not as their managers. They should therefore have access to easily understood information about the dynamics of the stress process and how it works. This enables them to see for themselves that the issue is a real one and worth addressing. It also provides a common language for talking about the issues as well as helping create an environment where stress is something that can be talked about.

In the work that we do with organisations we usually begin with an insight into the 'fight or flight' mechanism that is a natural part of our survival physiology. Using 'stress dots' – small skin thermometers that change colour depending on the level of tension felt by the wearer – we not only build participation in the session but also help employees to see for themselves that the stress reaction is normal and has some benefits.

All of this is aimed at making the employees feel more comfortable about the objectives for the survey. To build a sense that they are not being singled out as potential casualties, but that there are real benefits in the company knowing more about the amount of pressure they face and how they cope with it. As we said at the beginning of this book, we want to explain to everyone in the organisation that stress is not about being weak, it's about being human.

Managing expectations

In putting your message together, be honest about what can realistically be achieved as a result of the process. There will always be a good deal of employee scepticism about what will happen as a result of the survey. Some employees may have been involved in a survey that, despite all the hype at the beginning, seems to have led to no noticeable outcome.

If your company is guilty of this, make a point of acknowledging the fact that you have learnt from the past and be quite precise about what will happen as a result of this survey. That does not mean promising to make it all go away – few employees would believe that anyway. Instead what we find works best is an honest recognition that pressure is a feature of your business activity but that the company is interested in uncovering the areas where improvement is possible, as well as how they may be able to support them better.

Administering the audit

We have identified what it is we are trying to measure and we have identified who is going to be involved. We have communicated to both managers and employees what is going to happen, why we are doing it and what is involved for them. At last we are ready to send out a questionnaire!

Distribution

What format for the questionnaire?

Distributing the survey instrument can be done a number of ways. Traditionally, companies have distributed paper and pencil questionnaires, and despite the advance in electronic forms of communication, paper questionnaires are still favoured by many. They are very portable, instantly recognisable and preferred by many because they are so easy to use.

Increasingly though, many of the companies we work with are favouring electronic media, such as e-mail file attachments or intranet-delivered questionnaires. E-mail can have advantages over a paper-based approach in that the distribution is fast and immediate. It can, however, increase anxiety over confidentiality if the level of confidence in the security of the e-mail network is shaky in any way. Distributing diskettes offers more security and has the advantage, shared by e-mail-based approaches, of allowing people to enter their responses directly onto a computer file, which simplifies both the scoring and aggregation processes. Both of these approaches, however, necessitate employees having easy and uninterrupted access to a PC for a period of about 30 minutes, which can be a problem for some participants.

Intranet delivery is becoming a more popular option, with the added advantage that briefing materials and messages can also be placed alongside the questionnaire to remind people of the purpose of the survey and so on. As with e-mail and diskette delivery though, there will be issues for some around PC access and confidentiality.

The most appropriate method for your organisation will depend very much on the type of work and work pattern of the survey population. Clearly employees who operate in a technological environment or who are based at their own desk are probably not going to find an e-mail or intranet questionnaire a major challenge. Employees involved in manual jobs, or employees who travel a good deal of the time will probably find a paper questionnaire more manageable. There are benefits and drawbacks to each of the approaches so choose the method most suitable for the employees you are seeking to involve. The optimum solution is, of course, to have the questionnaire available in paper and electronic versions and let the participants choose!

Timing

Whatever the chosen method of asking the questions, the timing of the mailing is also an important consideration. Aside from avoiding major holidays, festivals and other corporate survey initiatives, the timing of the mailing should aim to be as close as possible to the pre-communication briefings. The smallest possible time lag will mean that the instrument reaches the recipients while they can still remember the answer to the question, 'what's in it for me?'. Leave it too long and the feeling will be that all the hype did not amount to very much after all.

Whilst mentioning previous survey work, it can be expected that many of the survey participants will have been asked to respond to another survey in the preceding 12 months. A degree of survey fatigue is always likely to be a factor for consideration. There are benefits, therefore, in either spacing the timing of a stress audit appropriately, or where the subject matter of previous initiatives allows, positioning the audit as a follow-on activity from previous work. This can be particularly beneficial if there is perceived to be a commonly held belief amongst employees that nothing ever happens as a result of 'all these surveys'.

Manager support

Once the questionnaires are in the workplace it is vital that managers are seen to visibly support the process. This means that they must complete their own questionnaires and encourage others to do so. Managers have to do more than just appear to support the process – they need to invest their own time and demonstrate that they feel this is a valuable and important piece of work for the company. One of the best ways they can achieve this is to formally set time aside to allow employees to complete the questionnaire.

Allocating work time

Whether there is a practical need to formally allocate time away from daily duties to attend a briefing session and subsequently complete the questionnaire will depend on the nature of the work being carried out. Whether it is practically necessary or not it is desirable to position the survey as a legitimate part of the working day and to advertise to employees that they should seek to complete it in company time. If the employee then prefers to complete it at home or in their own time that is a decision for them. We firmly believe that if management is not willing to allocate *work time* to the audit then they shouldn't undertake to do it.

In our experience employers who are not prepared to recompense people for the time they spend filling in the questionnaire are unlikely to take the results seriously or do anything with them. The audit process is for the benefit of both the individual and the organisation, and completing the questionnaire is a rightful part of the working day. Many people find that it's relatively easy to schedule time to complete the questionnaire but in more restrictive jobs this may not be possible and time needs to be built into the staffing rota. In some environments it may even be necessary to bring in temporary staff to cover work whilst the questionnaires are being completed. The highest response rates amongst survey populations that we have ever seen were achieved where line managers led the project and allocated specific times on particular days for each team to complete the questionnaire.

Getting the questionnaires back

As anyone involved in survey work will know, sending out a questionnaire is no guarantee of actually receiving a completed one back! As we discussed earlier in this chapter, maximising response rates is a function of making individuals feel interested in participating, reassuring them that their answers are confidential and making it easy to participate. In our experience the confidentiality issues can be addressed by giving individuals the opportunity to send their questionnaires back to an external provider of the service, but this is likely to have some cost implications. For organisations with a more trusting approach to management, a ballot-box system can work well. Completed questionnaires or disks are sealed in envelopes and sent through internal mail to a central contact, who is then responsible for sending them onward for processing.

Whichever method is adopted, it needs to be clear what the employee needs to do once they have completed the questionnaire. The most poorly organised cases we have seen often involve the employee in considerable work. One notable example required the employee to obtain a questionnaire by downloading a file attachment from an e-mail, saving to a disk, completing the questionnaire and hunting around for a stamp, the envelope and an address to return it to the external providers. In a pressured environment this would be one more daily hassle too many, with the response rate being a predictable casualty.

Helplines

It is worth enquiring whether the provider of the survey instrument is able to offer a helpline service to employees who may need clarification about a particular survey question or need another copy of the questionnaire. Our experience has been that this is a worthwhile service to make available, as there are often employees who genuinely want to participate but have a small concern that can be easily answered.

Where individual feedback is being provided it is in the company's interest to have as many people take part in the survey as possible. 'Losing' a responder because their pet ate the questionnaire at home is a real waste of an opportunity! Similarly, where e-mail, intranet delivery or computer disks are being used a helpline is a necessity, as a few people will inevitably experience technical difficulty accessing the necessary files. Interest in participating will soon wane if help is not at hand.

Reminder cycle

An important part of the distribution process is to schedule a reminder. We know from experience that many employees asked to participate in surveys fully intend to complete the questionnaire but forget, mislay the original questionnaire, start it and get distracted, and so on. A reminder letter to non-responders, or a global reminder to all advertising that the closing date is drawing closer, can have quite an impact on the overall response rates. Where a helpline is provided, a reminder often prompts a flurry of requests for additional questionnaires or clarification of small issues. Halfway through a survey there are invariably more interested parties than there are completed questionnaires.

Feedback

We shall be covering this area in more detail in Chapter 8, but it is important that we touch on the importance of employee feedback in this section on administering an audit. Looked at from the employee point of view, there have been a lot of words said and communication pieces circulated about the importance of the survey and what will follow as a result. This increase in noise about the issue, and the company's interest in it, will have reached a peak about the time they complete the questionnaire. Fired up by an effective pre-communication programme, the employee sends the questionnaire off for analysis and will more than likely expect a prompt reply. The reality is that processing, initial analysis, discussion groups to flesh out the findings and then final data analysis will usually take a little time. As a result there may be a significant time lag between completing the questionnaire and receiving either personal feedback or details of the aggregated results.

If it looks as if this is likely to be the case in your survey, it is well worth the trouble to remind employees that we are now entering the data analysis phase and that there will be "quiet time" between now and the feedback phase. This has the effect of both pre-empting concerns and inappropriate assumptions about corporate silence on the subject, and reinforcing that the company still has every intention of telling participants about the survey findings.

Participants should be reminded that the feedback will be in two forms. The first is likely to be their personal profile (if you are using an external provider and they are able to generate confidential individual results). The second is likely to be a company communication piece or briefing session that will enable them to see the aggregated findings and the action plan. If this detail is overlooked there is a danger that the survey will start to appear as though it has the same characteristics of other less interactive approaches – lots of noise and then no action!

EIGHT

Interpreting the
Information

Analysing the data – Can we trust it? What does it tell us?

If the survey has been carried out as described in the previous chapter then you should be able to trust the information you've got back from your staff. However, it is useful to be aware of the dangers inherent in surveys. You may have lots of interesting data but if it's not accurate or valid then, however sophisticated your data analysis and interpretation of the results, the survey will be useless.

Controlling for biased responses

One of the major concerns about interpreting the results of questionnaire-based surveys is the extent to which the results accurately reflect the feelings of the group. There are several different problems, all of which can come together in a badly designed and badly implemented survey to make the results much worse than useless. Bias can come from any or all of the following areas:

- Low response rates
- Motivational distortion
- Badly worded questions
- Superficial analysis – the danger of averages.

Low response rates

If only a small proportion of people – less than 40%, for example – complete the questionnaire then the results are unlikely to be representative of the whole. The problem is confounded because you don't know if the people who have bothered to reply are the most enthusiastic, happiest employees with no stress and lots of time to complete questionnaires. Alternatively your 40% could be the most stressed employees, desperate for any sort of lifeline and willing to give up their precious time because they have a vague hope that at last their couldn't-care-less managers will take some notice of how fed up they are. Quite a contrast, and in reality it will rarely be this clear-cut. However, with low response rates, how do you know which end of the spectrum you are sampling from? Does the data have a positively rose-coloured or stressed-out-black shade – or is it just muddy brown?

Motivational distortion

Motivational distortion occurs when people change the way that they answer the questions because they want to influence the outcome. If personality tests are being used as part of a selection process then some people may try to choose their answers to portray themselves in a more favourable light. To combat this, some selection questionnaires have built-in measures of motivational distortion designed to catch the fakers. In stress questionnaires the problem is exacerbated because people could try to 'fake good' as well as 'fake bad'. They may, for example, believe that if they make sure workload or rates of pay are a source of stress they could get more staff or more money. Other people, fearful of a negative response to a poor survey, would pretend everything was fine. An extreme but not unknown consequence of this type of 'faking bad' would be an employer closing down a plant because they felt the employees were too stressed to cope with any more change.

The way to eliminate this type of bias is to remove the desire to distort the answers. If there is no reason to falsify the response, there is no need to build in lie detector scales or motivational distortion measures. This, once again, comes back to the way the questionnaire is introduced into the organisation. The pre-audit communications and the briefing session must guarantee confidentiality. If people believe that their results could end up on their personnel file or be shown to their manager they will never give an honest answer.

Badly worded questions

Questionnaire design seems so easy, but is full of potential pitfalls. A common mistake made by people who write their own question- naires is to pay insufficient attention to the quality of their questions. We have seen numerous examples of questionnaires that have been administered to staff by the employer in which the questions are so ambiguous or confusing as to make any interpretation of the results meaningless. Writing items for questionnaires appears to be simple but each item needs to be checked, evaluated and analysed to ensure that the underlying constructs are clear and that the item is able to discriminate between employees in a meaningful way. For example if, on a one to six rating scale, everybody answers between four and six, then the item is not giving useful information and fails to capture the full range of feelings on the subject. Items such as 'I think my company is a great place to work' with answers on a one to six scale where one is 'it's good' and six is 'it's fabulous' obviously miss the point that many people may actively dislike working there!

We have been approached by far too many companies asking us to help them interpret data from their own questionnaires because they don't know what the results mean. It's very disappointing to have to explain that their data is useless because their questions don't measure what the company thinks they're measuring. It is therefore vitally important that the quality of your questions is good right from the start. You will need to assess whether or not you need external input to the content and phrasing of the questions you want to ask, or whether you would be better served by using a standardised questionnaire.

Superficial analysis – the danger of averages

As discussed in Chapter 6, beware of averages! (see Figures 8.1 and 8.2). An example of the danger of averages is the analysis of the data from a stress audit on a company's sales force. The audit was

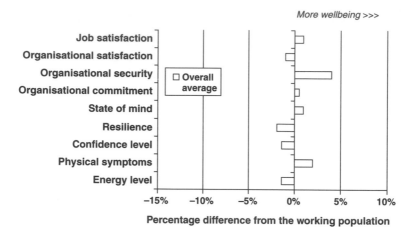

Figure 8.1 *Effects of stress – overall*

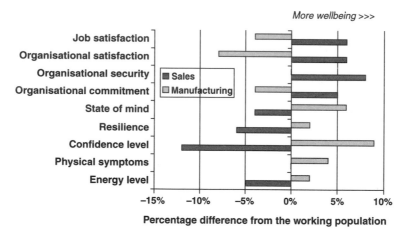

Figure 8.2 *Effects of stress – compared by workgroup*

administered to everyone in the sales force: managers, sales people and support staff. The overall average for the organisation was reasonably good and the first conclusion was that stress wasn't a major issue. However, more detailed analysis of the data showed that when the three groups – managers, sales and support staff – were compared with each other major differences appeared. The managers had excellent stress profiles, the support staff had average profiles and the sales people had very poor profiles. The analysis pinpointed specific issues facing the sales people that needed to be addressed as a matter of urgency. A simple overview would have missed the problem. Sometimes it's necessary to dig even further into the data to reveal specific groups of employees who have a problem. The issues may be so localised that the plight of a small group of people in one department of a regional office may be missed unless care is taken with the analysis. Of course there are limits to how finely the data can be cut. There could be breaches of confidentiality if the group size is too small and the smaller the number of people the less robust the average for the group. As a rule we do not analyse groups of fewer than 10 people.

Benchmarking

One of the most interesting benefits of a well-run audit is discovering the extent to which your organisation differs from other, similar organisations. The key question that needs to be addressed is: 'Compared with other organisations in our industry sector do we have a problem?' That is, 'Is occupational stress more or less of an issue for us than it is for our competitors?' Unfortunately the inability to be able to do effective benchmarking is the single biggest drawback for studies that do not make use of a standardised and well-used diagnostic tool.

If you decide to use a standardised questionnaire you should ask about the availability of the provider's database for benchmarking purposes. You should be most interested in finding out about their ability to benchmark against other companies in your industry. Whilst you should not expect to learn the names of other companies, you should be reassured that there is sufficient mass in the database for any comparison with your results to be both statistically significant and relevant. Obviously, the more relevant the benchmark data, the more useful the comparison. For example, in presenting the results of a stress audit to the IT managers of a large corporation, they were quite interested in the benchmark comparison with the working population. They liked being compared with other senior managers but the bit that really got them interested was when we benchmarked them against other senior IT people working in similar organisations. The relevance of benchmarking is very important; the more external benchmarks, the better. When it is possible to compare the business with similar businesses and then compare managers with managers at the same level, sales assistants with other sales assistants and so on, the analysis of differences and similarities is compelling. For example, in the public sector we look at a wide variety of jobs over a range of grades. The ability to be able to compare groups such as finance officers at a specific grade gives meaningful information on the nature and extent of stress, as well as key differences in the sources of pressure.

Discussion groups

The use of a survey instrument will provide a large volume of quantitative information for analysis. As we will shortly see, this data can be filtered, profiled, correlated, and cross-referenced to develop a detailed understanding of the 'what' and the 'where' of organisational stress issues. But, however sensitive your measurement approach, it will be difficult to capture the 'why' information. Trying to interpret raw survey data without a feeling for the context in which the information was gathered and the generally prevailing attitude towards the survey and the organisation is fraught with danger.

Empirical data is always open to a number of interpretations. Whilst it may be possible to draw upon your understanding of the context, attitudes and so on when analysing and reporting results, it is dangerous to do this without first checking your assumptions about the way participating employees view the organisation. The necessity for qualitative information does not to diminish the power in the raw data; it is a rich source of information in its own right. But in our experience the data really comes alive when it is combined with an understanding of the contextual issues. This rounds out our understanding of what the data patterns tell us as well as building confidence that the conclusions drawn are correct. We therefore strongly recommend that preliminary analysis of the data is carried out to establish the major indicators, and that this is then 'sense-checked' with groups of employees in a focus group environment.

What are the objectives of a focus group?

Focus group discussions are there to achieve two main objectives. The first of these has already been mentioned, that is to round out the information we already have about observable trends and attitudes. Gathering more qualitative information about the way that employees feel and why they believe the issues are real for them increases the probability that we can isolate and further analyse the issues that are practically as well as statistically significant. Encouraging employees to share their local experiences helps build a picture of why the results are emerging the way that they are. This knowledge will be vital when it comes to designing and then prioritising interventions.

This brings us to the second objective, namely to get a sense of where the participating employees perceive the most effective solutions might lie. Management textbooks are littered with advice to 'ask the people'. Most managers will recognise that they cannot possibly be close enough to every detail of day-to-day activity to be able to isolate the changes required with as much accuracy as the individuals affected by these changes can. The more senior the manager the more likely this is to be the case. In virtually all of our work the employees can articulate much more clearly than their supervisors and managers which developments in style, process, support and so on will make the greatest difference to them. What they see as making a difference is often wildly different from what the management teams anticipate the needs will be. The greatest convergence is usually to be found in the complexity of what is needed. The managers anticipate major re-engineering change. The employees often desire incremental adjustment. Often it is about a change in emphasis rather than a change in environment. These are important insights to capture. If the endgame of a stress audit is to make things better, and clearly it is, then not capturing this information is a risky strategy.

Who should attend a focus group?

We looked in Chapter 5 at who the company could choose to attend a discussion group. If the purpose here is to 'sense check' audit data then obviously you will want to include those who participated in the survey. Which individuals you choose from this group will, of course, be a local decision. There are, however, a few golden rules if the discussions are to be successful. They need to be attended by enough individuals to give a balanced view. This means ensuring that there are sufficient people in the room to facilitate open contribution and that those contributing represent a fair spread of those who can reasonably be anticipated to have knowledge, experience and attitudes towards the organisation that are robust and representative.

What to ask

Discussion groups should be used to flesh out or 'sense check' what your data seems to be telling you. This means therefore that you need to use the open style of questioning discussed in Chapter 5 to find out more of the background to some of the results that you see. Thus if your results suggest that there may be some issues around recognition you will want to ask questions like 'To what extent do you feel recognised for the contribution that you make?' or 'How do people get recognised in your part of the business/department?' Similarly if there appear to be some issues around leadership style then you might ask, 'How would you describe the style of management that you experience?' or more simply still, 'How are people managed?'

Remember that you are looking to capture the essence of what is said rather than the specific detail of one manager's strengths over their developmental needs! Thus if you get many different management styles fed back to you, some of which are more supportive than others, then the learning is that there is variability between two polarities. If you can then explore the way in which people feel themselves to be affected by these differing styles then you have a clearer understanding of the source of the effects and most importantly which behaviours may need to be changed if there is to be progress. As we said in Chapter 5, it is important to keep probing for participants' sense of what would make the situation better, and many of your questions will need to be in this area. So, returning to our leadership style example, a follow-up question that you might direct towards those reporting dissatisfaction with the style of leadership might be 'How would you like to be managed?' 'What small behaviour change from your manager would make the biggest difference?'

How to organise focus groups

Discussion groups organised as a follow-up to a quantitative survey should be pulled together using the same guidelines as those detailed in Chapter 5. The only additional point to note is that the bulk of the attendees should be people who actually participated in the survey. If you have two different populations you obviously cannot combine the two sets of results in the same way. That does not mean that people who did not fill in a questionnaire should be excluded; in fact it is a good idea to get a few of these people to come along as well if you can. They can often offer some interesting insights about why they did not participate or why they believe other people may have decided not to.

Pulling the two sets of information together

Look for the areas where the qualitative feedback matches that of the quantitative. Look and take note of the areas where there seems to be a contradiction – this may suggest that some of your questions are not actually measuring what you hoped they might.

In our experience, there is usually a great deal of congruence between the findings of the focus groups and those of the question-naire data. In combination, the whole is much greater than the sum of the parts and maximises the benefit of each of these individually valid methods of data collection.

NINE

What Do I Do About the Issues?

Awareness – Responsibility – Action (ARA): Three-point Framework

Moving from an analysis of the issues to acting upon them requires a strategic rather than a tactical approach. Sending out a batch of questionnaires without appropriate employee pre-communication can weaken the effectiveness of your measurement. In the same way leaping into intervention without some degree of groundwork can seriously undermine the value of the data collection.

Our experience tells us that there is a three-stage strategic framework to be adopted that increases the probability that the hard work put into measurement gets translated into appropriate action.

Raising awareness

The first part of the strategic framework is raising awareness. We're concerned about pressure and stress in the workplace. If our investigation tells us there is a problem, the first thing we have to do is to help raise awareness of it and change both management and employee perception. We need to increase the level of understanding about the issue until it becomes clear that it's something legitimate that individuals and their employers can talk about. As long as the issue is buried under the carpet and managers and their staff dare not say anything about it, they will never make any progress in managing it. Raising awareness then has much to do with changing employee and manager perception and challenging 'old thinking' about stress as the price people pay for demonstrating their commitment and dedication. Stress should be seen as the unwanted and undesirable outcome of too much pressure, and not as a badge of commitment!

The change in attitude involves sending consistent messages around the organisation that there is an acceptance that life can often be difficult, work is frequently demanding and that some people suffer as a result. We shouldn't deny that people suffer from stress and we shouldn't pretend that there are easy answers. Instead the messages should revolve around our recognition that stress is an issue, and give a commitment that we will work together to establish how we will deal with it.

Providing honest and detailed information about the level of individual and organisational stress acts to increase understanding and awareness of the problem. Without awareness of the real issues, the process of effective, sustainable change cannot begin.

Accepting responsibility

The second part of the strategic framework is responsibility. One of the basic principles of occupational health management is that employees should not leave their workplace in a worse state of health than when they arrived. It is well accepted that people should not be made ill by their work and that employers have a duty of care towards their employees. The management of mental health risks is, therefore, as much a part of employer responsibility as concern for the physical and environmental safety of the workplace. The obvious difficulty in exercising this responsibility is that mental health risks are much more difficult to identify than an unguarded piece of machinery or a trailing wire.

There needs to be a shared understanding of who is responsible for managing work-related stress. Once a line manager or senior executive has become aware that there is pressure and stress within the organisation they need to know who is responsible for it. Should the employee do something about it or is it the employer's fault and therefore management that carries all the responsibility?

Alternatively the management team may believe that stress has little or nothing to do with work and it's up to employees to sort themselves out. In order to act on the information gained from investigating stress we need to know who is responsible for acting on the information. Is it management, employees or both? Where does responsibility really lie?

Clearly the employer has a duty to provide a safe working environment and ensure that the employees' psychological wellbeing is as well protected as their physical wellbeing. The legislative framework is becoming increasingly clear on the subject and, as we have already seen, if organisational causation can be established then there are a growing number of landmark cases to demonstrate that the employer can be held liable for personal injury to the employee. Wherever possible, therefore, stress must be dealt with at source and this would be deemed to be the employer's responsibility.

However, we believe that managing stress at work is also the responsibility of the individual employee. Each employee should take care of their own welfare and take steps to ensure that they are not subjecting themselves to unnecessary risk. If this is the case, to what extent does the employee's life outside of the workplace and their individual personality characteristics affect their potential to be damaged by the work we ask them to do? Where do my responsibilities as an employer end and theirs begin?

These are difficult questions to answer, and specialists in employment law have spent many hours working through the arguments. In advance of their judgement though, one thing does become clear. It's important to accept that responsibility for employee wellbeing cannot be delegated to the relevant professionals – the HR people, the welfare officers, occupational health and counselling staff. These professionals can advise and develop policy, but they cannot and should not replace each manager's responsibility for the wellbeing of their staff.

What emerges is that there is a shared responsibility for the issue of stress at work. From a practical perspective we do not need to know precisely where corporate responsibility ends and personal responsibility begins. At this stage all we need to recognise is that the responsibility is shared. Employee, line manager, chief executive, occupational health and human resource professionals all have a role to play in the effective management of occupational stress. With shared understanding of the issue, it is possible to define different, but strategically aligned, roles for each of the relevant parties that will protect the other from avoidable damage. Each of these individuals carries personal responsibility for doing what they can to reduce workplace stress.

Taking action

The third step in our strategic framework is taking action. We know that something needs to be done and where responsibility lies for doing it. Now we need to decide what we should do and, most importantly, make sure we do it!

We illustrate this stage in the framework with an analogy about crossing the road. Imagine that you're walking across the road and there's a bus coming towards you. You know that bus-drivers are incredibly well trained and very alert. So, you're in the middle of the road, can see the bus coming and you're aware now that there is a threat, and there is a danger. You may decide that because bus-drivers have been trained to avoid running people over, it's not really your responsibility to do anything about it; 'The bus-driver is responsible for avoiding me.' That's probably not a very sensible action. You may be safer if you assume that even if the bus driver does try to avoid you, you should get out of the way anyway. However, even if you accept full responsibility but don't do anything to change your situation then you're as dead as if you'd never seen the bus in the first place.

It's like this with stress at work, organisations, managers and employees need to be aware that stress at work is a real threat but, with appropriate action, it can be avoided. Depending on the nature of the problem and the specific cocktail of pressures the primary responsibility may lie with management or with the individual employee. In most cases both can do something about it. But if they aren't aware of the problem or have no idea that it's fixable then they are powerless to act. If they realise that there is a problem and still don't do anything differently, then the employee will be as ill or as stressed as if they hadn't noticed the problem in the first place. The effective management of workplace stress moves from awareness to action. One is of limited value without the other. Taking action to manage stress has to be done at as many levels as possible. The line manager shouldn't delay taking action until the corporate policy has been approved and shouldn't try to pass responsibility on to the professional advisors. Other people, such as senior managers and specialist advisers, should be involved as appropriate but, if there is evidence to show that an individual employee is suffering, then action should be taken without delay. Waiting to ask a policeman for his advice about how to avoid being run over by a bus may be a sensible precaution but it is not the best strategy for survival when the bus is about to hit you!

The link between awareness and action is one of the guiding principles behind our approach to the effective measurement and management of stress. Your new-found awareness and the deeper understanding you have gained through measurement is of limited value if there is no action. It's only when real understanding is coupled with appropriate and targeted interventions that progress is made. Investigation must be followed by intervention if it is to be of any value.

Sharing information with others

We have said that the questionnaire is not the audit. The questionnaire is the means of gathering the data but it is not the end in itself. In many respects it is the reporting phase that is the start of the stress management process.

There are three forms of feedback that need to be considered and we shall cover each of them in this chapter.

1. Feedback to the individual about the individual;
2. Feedback to managers about work group and company-wide data; and

3. Feedback to employees about the aggregated data and the action plan.

Feedback to the individual about the individual

Role of ARA framework at the individual level

In our view any detailed stress audit, requiring individual employees to give close consideration to the way they feel about work pressures and their capacity to deal with the issues they face, should deliver personal and confidential feedback to that individual. We find over and over again that individual employees derive enormous benefit from being able to read and act upon a personal pressure management profile. This personal feedback enables them to understand and deal with their specific issues without having to wait for management or organisational initiatives. It should give people appropriate and practical guidance on how they may be able to improve their situation. Even if stress is not a major issue, most people welcome the opportunity to improve their ability to manage pressure. In cases where the individual has serious problems with stress, either work- or home-related, the profile provides a clear indication of the need to seek further help and promotes early treatment. Of course, it is essential that the feedback they receive should be accurate, valid and reliable. A great deal of harm can be done by using inappropriate questionnaires or flawed interview techniques that may result in people being given inaccurate or inappropriate feedback. In an area as sensitive as stress or mental health you must ensure the quality of the information you give to your staff.

It is clear that it is going to be practically impossible for home-grown questionnaires to do this well enough for the information to be of real use. It is often for this reason that companies abandon attempts at a self-developed questionnaire in favour of an instrument that has been specifically designed to deliver relevant information back to both the employee and the employer. In many cases, constraints on finances or resources make it difficult to use a standardised, reliable instrument that provides high-quality individual feedback. This should not prevent you working with employees at an individual level but you should be aware of the issues so that by understanding what is missing from in house questionnaires you can introduce alternative steps to compensate for the lack of personal feedback.

The reason we believe personal feedback is so important is that we know the process of completing a stress questionnaire raises awareness of the issue. Providing personal reports to individuals in the way we have described not only supplies each employee with a detailed analysis of their stress profile, but also builds on the awareness already raised by the audit process. Appropriate feedback can encourage and enable them to take action straight away in areas that are relevant to them.

Providing information to individuals to help them manage their own situation more effectively does not absolve managers from their responsibility for primary prevention. It does, however, enable a two-pronged approach to improving the situation. As we have said, responsibility for stress at work is a shared responsibility. Providing personal feedback to individuals as part of the survey process is a valuable way of facilitating and enabling their contribution to the management of the issue. In time a thorough analysis of the aggregate data will further raise awareness at the organisational level and enable managers to take responsibility for work-related pressures. You will then have a joined-up approach with both parties working together.

This is not the way that most surveys or audits are run. Sadly in practice very few organisation-wide questionnaires or surveys do actually provide feedback to the individual. However, in a book whose purpose is detailing a best practice blueprint, the point needs to be made that personal feedback should be offered if you can structure your audit in that way. Our experience is that so much benefit is lost if feedback is not given. It would be unthinkable to put employees through a risk assessment such as assessing exposure to asbestosis and not tell them the results, so why do so many organisations do this with workplace stress? Do not underestimate the value of using individual feedback to prompt personal action. In almost every survey in which we have been involved, personal feedback has helped at least one individual employee to prevent a major breakdown by providing a mechanism for early detection and a prompt for early intervention.

The process that enables people to gain an insight into their problems and seek help usually requires little outside intervention, although counselling may obviously be necessary for the most extreme cases. Because the information and the interventions are at an individual level, they can take place within days or weeks of the questionnaires being completed. Both the individual employee and their organisation achieve a quick win and they see the benefits even before the organisation data has been analysed. In our experience the benefits of individual feedback are often overlooked but the advantages of working at both the individual and the organisational level are so great that it is much better to carry out a formal audit designed to give people feedback and provide the at-risk employees with a professional support service.

What might the personal feedback look like?

One example of a widely used, industry-standard pressure measurement questionnaire is the Pressure Management Indicator (the PMI). An integral feature of the PMI is a report writing system that generates a detailed personal profile giving relevant feedback to each individual who completes the questionnaire. As we have already discussed, this level of individual reporting is not usually possible with an in-house produced questionnaire. However, by describing the way the reports are used it may be possible to use a similar approach to guide a more informal discussion of workplace stress.

The PMI personal profile generator

The PMI scoring system produces an individual narrative report for each respondent. This 12-page report is generated by the expert system to give people an overall picture of their stress profile. It starts by describing the model of stress on which the PMI is based and then analyses each of the dimensions in detail. The report starts with an assessment of the effects of stress, and then covers the sources of pressure and individual differences. Finally, the report makes suggestions for improvement and, if appropriate, recommends a follow-up interview to explore any indications of stress-related illness.

Everyone who takes part in an audit process where the PMI is used as the core measurement tool is sent a personal report in a sealed envelope addressed to their home or work address. They are also offered the opportunity to talk to a counsellor or other suitably qualified advisor about the information provided in their report.

Understanding personal profiles

When people receive their profile they are asked to think about four questions designed to help them to make most use of the information.

- Do you have a problem?

  Is your current state of mental and physical wellbeing and your levels of satisfaction with the job and organisation OK?

- If there is a problem, what's causing it?

  Check your sources of pressure. Are there any demands that are significantly higher than others? Is the main source of pressure coming from home, or work, or a combination of the two? Is it coming from something not covered by the questionnaire? If so, where do you think it comes from?

- Is anything making the situation worse?

  Is there anything about your behavioural style or level of control that amplifies or moderates the pressure?

- How are you coping with the pressure?

  Are you using a broad range of coping and support skills? What more could you be doing to improve your ability to manage pressure?

An example of a PMI report can be found in the Appendix.

Further help – providing a safety net

Whether or not you are able to provide written personal feedback as part of the process, it is important to think through how people who have participated in the survey can gain further help if they think they need it. As we have already said, participation in a survey does much to raise awareness of the issues for all concerned. We have seen many cases of people who have been privately struggling with issues that have become much more real for them when asked specific questions about how they feel on these subjects. Some organisations have used this fact as a reason for inactivity; fearful that if they ask questions people will uncover issues that they did not know they had. In our experience, this is not how it happens. The process of enquiry, as we have said already, merely turns on the light – the metaphorical bodies were already on the floor. Failing to switch the light on does not mean that the problems are not there. Raising awareness can be the first step towards improvement if you can create an environment where people feel confident to talk to others about the concerns they have. It is also an excellent opportunity to reach people when their problems are still easily managed. The earlier people with stress problems seek help the faster and simpler the recovery.

If you are providing personal feedback then it is important to recognise that there may be some individuals who have received news about themselves they did not anticipate and who may therefore benefit from further advice. This may take the form of talking through the profile results, querying a part of its conclusions or even helping an employee to realise that they might benefit from more formal counselling.

It is important, therefore, to anticipate that this need may arise before the profiles are sent out, in order that those who want more information or help can access these services quickly and easily. Many organisations that we work with are fortunate to have in-house occupational health services. Where these resources are available it is a good idea to encourage employees who want to talk more about their profile or personal circumstances to access these confidential services. Including a covering letter with the profile, thanking them for their participation in the survey and directing them towards further support, can most effectively do this. Directing employees towards an existing employee assistance programme or external counselling provider is another route where there are no dedicated resources available internally.

The availability of support or counselling services is important for everyone who has completed a questionnaire. However, from our experience we know that in all survey populations there will be a small percentage of people whose questionnaire scores indicate that they are suffering mental health problems equal to or worse than those of psychiatric out-patients. The issue of getting help to those who really need it becomes even more acute for this section of the survey group. Issues of confidentiality will always surface when you think through how to offer help to people who really need it, and may need it urgently. The basic principle behind voluntary partici-pation in surveys, of course, is that you can only make it possible for people to seek further help. You cannot make them seek it. If you out-sourced your stress audit (as many do for reasons of confiden-tiality alone) then you will not know who falls into this category. It is vital that these people are made aware that help is available to them if they want it. Once again they can be given the information about where to seek this help in a non-intrusive way through careful advertisement of the service in a standard letter that accompanies the personal feedback. Choose your words carefully, as the least favourable outcome is that the person feels they have been singled out and that somehow the company 'knows'. We have found that including a paragraph at the end of the letter reminding people to take a copy of their profile to show whoever they see because they will not have a copy, provides some reassurance in this regard. This is particularly effective if people are being directed towards in-house resources.

Even if you are not able to provide personal feedback, you still need to make it clear where people can self-refer if they want to talk about stress and pressure. To reiterate a point made earlier, participation in a stress audit raises awareness. You have a golden opportunity at this point to advertise help in order to deliver it to people who could benefit the most. Posters, global e-mails, loose leaflets in coffee areas and so on, advertising the availability of whatever help you can supply, could be just the right message at the right time for one person. If you can motivate just one person to take action they might not have otherwise taken at that time, then you will have made a difference.

Feedback to managers about work group and company-wide data

One of the basic principles of running a stress survey is that you shouldn't ask the questions unless you are prepared to do something with the information. Feeding the results back to managers is the opportunity to start the transition from awareness to action. It is the point at which managers should begin the process of doing something to address the problems. With this in mind it is essential that the feedback of results is put in the context of a 'so what are we going to do about this?' meeting. Workplace stress surveys can generate an enormous amount of information and it is easy to fall into the trap of presenting too much detail in too much complexity. We've learned the hard way that showing 100 PowerPoint slides to a group of senior executives is not necessarily the most effective way of getting something done, however fascinating the data!

So keep the presentation simple, make sure that you highlight the key facts and that the background to the survey is well understood. At this stage your objective is to work with the group to identify the issues that they can do something about. This may involve a series of presentations to different groups of managers working with these groups on their specific issues. We have already discussed the danger of averages and the need to drill down into the data to find out exactly what the survey is telling you about different parts of the business. Use this approach to lead sessions that get as many groups of managers as possible involved in taking action.

As an example we would normally start the feedback process with an overview presentation to the senior management or leadership team. This would show the overall results for the workplace and, by looking at some of the subgroups, show the extent to which there are issues that need to be addressed across the workplace. These common issues are the responsibility of the leadership team and they should identify actions that need to be taken to start the process of improvement. The presentation should also show the diversity within the workplace and highlight issues that will need to be addressed at a workgroup or local management level. We would like the senior management team to be aware of local issues and actively support local initiatives but feel that specific actions should be agreed lower down the organisation.

Work group reports

Revealing information about workgroups can be difficult, particularly if there is a tendency to blame or penalise individual managers because their groups are more stressed than others. Some organisations see comparisons by workgroups as a league table of success and failure with the implied assumption that the groups with the highest levels of stress have the worst managers. Even though this may sometimes be true, it isn't always the case and, in any event, this attitude isn't conducive to constructive debate. What we prefer to do is to show the senior management team information about the variability of results by workgroup so that they can see – for example, in a call centre – that there is a 60 percentile-point difference in pressure from relationships at work between customer service teams. The people making up these teams are doing the same job in the same location under the same conditions. The results clearly show enormous variability in the way they are managed and, in this case, highlight the need to improve supervisory skills. Knowing the range of scores helps senior managers to see that this is a workgroup, not a company-wide, issue; and encourages them to consider making resources available to support the team leaders.

The individual team leaders are then given a confidential workgroup report that they can use to see where they stand in relation to the other team leaders. There is no league table of success but each team leader has relevant information about their workgroup that they can use as part of their personal development programme.

Feedback to employees

It's good practice to make sure before the survey starts that the organisation is committed to releasing and sharing the information with the people who take part in the study. We know of organisations that spend significant amounts of time, money and resources to carry out a stress audit without having thought through how and with whom they will share the results. If these organisations don't share the results they run the risk of raising expectations amongst their staff that they cannot meet and, as a result, end up with a more disillusioned and dissatisfied workforce. Our advice is simple: if you're not prepared to share the results – don't do the survey!

When people are asked to take part in the audit they should be told that a summary of the overall group results will be made available to all employees either through a written summary report or briefing sessions. Where possible the summary report should be supplemented with an action list from the organisation saying what action they will take as a result. Making it clear from the outset that the results will be shared is a powerful motivator. It underlines the importance of open communications and reinforces three key messages:

- We're taking this seriously.
- We have nothing to hide.
- We're acting on the results.

The best-practice way of providing feedback to the employees is to make sure that everybody has the opportunity to understand the key messages in the overall report. This means that the main findings and, if available, the recommendations for action should be shared with all employees in a straightforward, easy-to-understand way. Some companies we work with hold briefing sessions to feed back the results and answer questions. Others send out summary reports, some others post the information on the corporate intranet. A few do all three! Whichever method you choose, the key point is to maintain and enhance management's creditability and honesty in the process. Do what you said you were going to do. Share the information, however unpalatable; remember your staff know it anyway! And, most importantly, get people involved in finding solutions. Use the results to trigger participation in working together to solve a common problem.

TEN

Levels of Intervention

So far we have focused our attention on measurement. This is to be expected as accurate diagnosis before intervention is the major platform in best-practice stress management. But as our three-stage strategic framework has made clear, accurate measurement only gives us increased awareness. On its own this is not enough, as awareness without effective action will not produce sustainable change.

Ultimately proactive stress management is stress prevention wherever possible, combined with and supplemented by behaviour changes that build the ability to cope with pressure. In practice a lot of stress management in companies today does neither of these and focuses instead on 'repairing' the casualties of workplace stress through counselling and advice.

Treating the casualties is one form of intervention, but it is not one that this chapter will say too much about, as it is at the wrong end of the prevention spectrum. Best practice dictates that prevention is better than cure – and prevention usually involves somebody doing something differently. We want to talk more about how companies can use their new-found awareness of the real issues to drive change that will reverse some of the negative effects of pressure in their workplace to produce positive morale, satisfaction and employee health outcomes.

Dealing with the issues at source to prevent the occurrence of stress is what is known as 'primary intervention'. It is the most fundamental level of the three types of stress management intervention.

Primary, secondary and tertiary intervention

Primary intervention

This seeks to remove or moderate the effect of stress by removing or moderating the source of the problem. Typically in organisational stress management this will involve management style or processes.

Secondary intervention

This leaves the source of the problem unaddressed but seeks to moderate or remove the impact on the employee by enhancing their capacity to cope. Returning to the four-way dynamic model of stress for a moment, this is the equivalent of developing an individual's ability to adapt and become resilient to pressure, thus effectively counterbalancing the pressure itself. This is usually achieved through training workshops.

Tertiary intervention

Tertiary intervention deals with the treatment of someone who is already suffering from stress. The purpose of tertiary intervention is to heal a damaged individual and increase their capacity to cope with stress, rather than prevent it.

What intervention?

It should be clear from these short summary details of each of the types of intervention that a string of tertiary interventions does not amount to proactive management of stress at work. That said, a focus solely on primary intervention would not necessarily address all the issues. However good your primary prevention, some individuals may still experience stress, and a strategic approach to the issue will need to make some provision for this.

Similarly, building individual coping capacity by focusing purely on secondary intervention does not constitute an integrated approach to stress management. The employer has a duty of care to manage risks in the workplace, and eradicating mental health risks at source is clearly the best place to start.

Best practice in stress management is therefore likely to involve a combination of all three approaches – different activities of each type can then combine to form an integrated whole that addresses the different drivers. With a combined approach the organisation can:

- Remove the problem at source by addressing as many of the organisational issues as commercially possible (primary intervention).
- Equip individuals to handle pressure so that wherever possible the outcome from a spell outside of their personal 'comfort zone' results in growth and not stress (secondary intervention).
- Provide 'emergency' services for those whose combination of circumstances either at work or at home results in them becoming ill.

Effective intervention is therefore matched to real needs – that have been identified and clarified through the audit process. Awareness is then tied to action that addresses both the causes and the outcomes.

However, in any discussion about intervention we are going to have to revisit the concept of responsibility. As our three-stage strategic framework made clear – awareness does not of itself lead automatically to action. Actions have to be identified and initiated. This means someone or some people need to accept responsibility for the appropriate intervention.

Whose problem is this anyway?

It is a generalisation, but it is worth remembering, that the default position taken on this by almost everybody will be, 'It is somebody else's problem.' This is not usually because of a lack of interest in the subject or in finding a solution. The attitude stems from a belief that the reason I can't do anything is because I need other people to do something first, 'I cannot fix this until they fix that.' The most common manifestation of this attitude is middle managers' refusal to do something until their bosses sort things out first. Making progress with challenging this belief is a major part of driving effective intervention. Helping individuals and managers to see that *they* need to take control and act has, in our experience, the biggest payback in terms of accelerating change. Waiting for others to 'get their house in order' is the fastest route to no progress at all.

Linked to this concept of personal responsibility is another big intervention question – who decides what we do?

Who decides what we do?

If we know *what* the issues are and we know *which* part of the business is most affected then who specifically do we make responsible for identifying and implementing the required changes? Is it a board decision? Is it a general or local management decision? What about the team members themselves – might they have an insight?

In theory there are very many people who, given sight of the results, will be able to tell you 'what we need to do'. But when it comes to identifying the *right* intervention, all our experience has taught us that the best possible people to get involved are from the teams who reported the issues in the first place. Far too many investigations into stress fail at the action stage because, having read the results, the managers decide what needs to be done without recourse to the team members themselves. Tablets of stone are handed down and invariably stay metaphorically propped up against the wall. Few interventions that start life this way ever get to implementation. The teams on the receiving end have no commitment to them and often cannot see the connection between the responses they gave to the survey and how this is going to make it better. There is quite simply too big a gap between the issue and the response.

We have a phrase that we use to help our clients avoid this mistake and that is: 'get the people involved in being involved.' Involving the staff in the identification of interventions is the smartest move you can make. It works not just because they know better than anyone what will make a difference to how they feel, but also because the very process of being involved feeds a basic need for some influence, however small, over their working lives. Getting people involved in the identification of the appropriate intervention builds their interest in and commitment to seeing the necessary changes through. This approach seems so obvious to us we fail to understand why so few organisations use it.

There is another reason for getting the people involved and fostering a sense of shared responsibility for change right from the very beginning of the intervention phase. The 'I can't fix this until they have fixed that' syndrome is not just a management phenomenon. People on the ground feel this just as much, probably more so, than most members of the management team and very often for good reason. In a working environment where there are few opportunities for control or influence over the way work is organised, it is not surprising that people do not feel able to change things for themselves. We very often meet resistance in workshops to the idea that 'managers aren't going to fix this for you' and that the delegates have a responsibility to meet their managers in the middle by changing their behaviour where they can and driving change form the 'bottom up'. Not surprisingly the more autocratic the management style the stronger and more entrenched is this way of thinking. An important part of making progress, though, is to challenge this way of approaching issues. You will need to take steps to create and then develop an environment where people can help themselves and each other. Openly sharing survey results and encouraging them to work as a group to identify their own list of possible interventions sends a very strong message of 'this is a shared responsibility' and fits perfectly with the final message: 'You have some control.'

In thinking about intervention, this concept of shared responsibility is key. As we saw when we looked at the different types of intervention, there are areas that the organisation can take responsibility for and areas where the individual may also have to change behaviour or do things differently.

The Intervention Model

In practice each layer of intervention involves separate but related responsibilities on both the organisation and the individual. Looking at Figure 10.1 there are both personal and organisational responsibilities in primary intervention. The organisation may need to examine issues such as management style; the individual might need to examine whether they routinely over-commit in terms of what they can realistically deliver. In secondary intervention the organisation may need to provide training and development in general coping and resilience skills; the individual will need to make an effort to implement and use the skills to which they have been exposed. Even with tertiary intervention the responsibilities are shared. The organisation can take care to provide support and counselling for people with advanced stress issues, but if the individual does not access them or implement the approaches suggested to them during the sessions, then no progress will be made. Similarly, if the individual who has stress issues does make use of the support services available but nothing is done by the organisation to address the work-related issues that created the need to seek help, then once again there would be no lasting progress. Making lasting progress requires the joint co-operation of employees

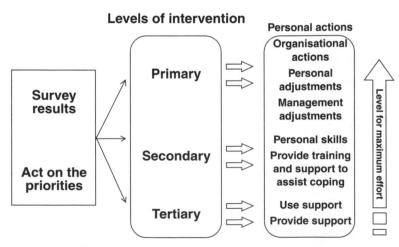

Figure 10.1   *Three types of intervention*

and the management team. The contribution of one party is no good without the other!

In Chapter 5 we spoke of the importance of gaining middle management buy-in to the survey process and the reason for this should by now be very clear. Managers who were involved from the start will have a more well-developed sense of ownership of the results when they become known. As a result they are going to have more commitment to defining and then owning their share of responsibility for the interventions. This is where the effort devoted to getting people on board will pay off. Conversely this is the stage where it will become obvious that the buy-in was not really there if this stage in the process was skimped. However, if you did your groundwork well then gaining management buy-in to action should not be too much of a problem.

However, building individuals' awareness of their responsibilities towards change, as we have said, can be challenging! As we saw before there is a natural tendency for people to place their responsibilities safely behind someone else's in a never-ending queue of things waiting to happen. In addition to this many will see the issues that drive the results as big and complicated and frankly unmanageable, leading to the conclusion that 'Oh yes – well, we know *that* but it has always been the same and there is nothing we can do to change it.'

We call this the 'big problem focus' and it can, on the face of it, be a hard nut to crack. It is true; many of the issues that you will uncover may appear to be big issues that are 'hard-wired' into the way the business is put together and which may on the surface appear to be fixed and immovable. But do not lose your faith! Even big issues have small components and the ability to challenge assumptions about some of the big issues and get to some of the constituent parts is the key to making sustainable progress .

These themes of personal control, accepting responsibility and looking for change on the ground form an integrated approach to finding practical solutions that are simple and cost-effective to implement. This is the key to making real progress.

Three big wins in one

The rest of this chapter will be devoted to a series of techniques that can be employed by staff to help them work with survey results and identify what can be done to make things better. Designed to be used in a small group environment, these approaches will enable team members and their managers to uncover together how they can make progress with the issues, irrespective of whether these are large or small.

Getting small groups to work together on the issues in this way delivers results because it

- develops a sense of personal control and involvement;
- increases the probability that the right interventions will be identified; and
- builds ownership of those interventions and 'enlightened self-interest' in making sure they are implemented.

The power embedded in this approach is that it delivers three big wins in one. It is a first step in its own right, independent of anything that might be identified and subsequently implemented as a result of the work itself. Getting teams involved in being involved produces the right answers faster than anything that could be grown in the boardroom, and much more besides!

Prompt interventions

The next step in a successful intervention strategy is to keep the momentum going. Show your staff that you've listened and are responding by doing something fast. As detailed in Chapter 7, part of the communication messages preceding an audit should be that the last part of the process will be the implementation of prompt interventions. We said then that, whilst it is not possible to second-guess what will be revealed by the audit, it is desirable to make a commitment to implement at least one change very soon after the survey has been completed and the results fed back. The commitment to act is therefore as fundamental a part of the project planning process as sending out the questionnaires. But having made that commitment it is of course essential that it is carried out.

Prompt intervention is necessary because if there are no observable signs of change as a result of the survey, then all the words said in the pre-communication briefings, and all the management support given to the process, will appear to have amounted to very little. This is why we say you must be prepared to act before you audit. Measurement raises expectations and if you have generated enthusiasm for the audit process you need to demonstrate just as much commitment towards working with the results, however unpalatable they may be.

The good news is that the results are rarely as frightening as people imagine. That is not to say that employers are consistently surprised that they have no pressure management issues – this is not the case. But what they are often pleased to find is that the sources of the problem are more easily remedied than they thought. There are usually one or two obvious 'quick wins' that can be communicated and implemented to 'buy time' for working on some of the thornier issues.

Raising awareness leads to action – the manager's case study

A senior manager completed his PMI as part of a stress audit in his department. His personal profile showed that he had been working very hard, focusing on his job and neglecting himself and his family. Since joining the organisation two years earlier, he had been working extremely long hours and, trying to cope with ever-increasing pressure of work, had missed holidays and worked many weekends. The PMI profile acted as a prompt. It made him realise that his life was out of balance. It was, in his words, like holding up a mirror and seeing what a terrible mess he was in. He had been so busy doing the job he hadn't thought about himself or the impact of his work on his family, and hadn't realised that stress was an issue.

Once he realised that he'd ignored his personal wellbeing he decided to take responsibility for improving his stress profile. So he did a couple of very simple things. His first action was to book a holiday for himself and his family and go on it without taking a briefcase full of work with him or ringing the office while he was away. This in itself started shifting control from his work to his life. Actually taking the holiday was a significant step. He had booked holidays before but had then cancelled them because work had been too demanding. 'Sorry,' he'd say to his family. 'I can't go now. There's something very important happening at work. We'll do it later – when it gets a bit easier.'

The second thing he did was to book himself on a time-management and delegation skills course. He realised the lack of such skills was a weakness in his management style and was probably one of the major reasons he never seemed to be able to deal with his workload. He couldn't see an easy way to reduce the work coming in but he could appreciate that he could manage it more effectively.

When we measured the department again a few months later, we found some very positive changes. The senior manager's profile had improved dramatically. The manager hadn't set himself up to fail by setting unrealistic targets for change. He had understood the need for sustainable improvements. For example, he set himself a goal of leaving earlier but limited it to three nights a week. Instead of saying 'I've got to go home at 4 p.m. or 5 p.m. every day', he told his staff, 'I'm going to try and get home by 6.30 p.m. three nights a week.' He also decided that he would only work every other weekend.

The manager made a significant improvement in his life that was measured by the change in his PMI profile when he redid the questionnaire six months later. In addition, the stress profiles of his staff also improved. Instead of him doing everything, he delegated more and gave his people more responsibility. The delegation skills training provided the techniques he knew he had to learn in order to improve his ability to manage pressure. The questionnaire provided the impetus for change and helped him to focus on specific issues that he could address. He could have gone on a training course at any time in the past but it probably wouldn't have been that helpful. The results of the questionnaire gave him the motivation to change and highlighted what he needed to do differently.

This is a good example of a senior manger using his position in the company to make big changes to the way he and his team worked. The intervention didn't require a special budget or a series of meetings or a formal project plan. It was a simple response to an identified need that, quite correctly, was dealt with within normal management practices.

The other point to make about this case study is that everyone can make some changes in their lives to improve their ability to manage pressure. You don't have to be a manager to make a difference. All employees, at whatever level, can make small changes in their working lives to make things a bit easier for them. It's really trying to say, 'Let's use the information in the profile to see if there is anything I can do differently to manage my pressure more effectively.' In our experience just going through the thought processes and finding one little improvement can have a very positive outcome.

ELEVEN

Summary

Prepare to succeed

Managing a stress audit is like painting a house. The end result depends on the quality of the preparation. If the preparation is skimped then the end result will suffer. Layers of paint will not hide a badly prepared surface. The sanding is more important than the painting and a good decorator will probably spend far longer preparing the surfaces than applying paint, and in a stress audit it's the quality of the preparation that makes the difference. It's the effort and thought that goes into marketing the audit and briefing the staff. It's making sure that people in the organisation understand the process and get the right messages so that they are not worried about issues such as confidentiality. The briefing and pre-audit communication should give them clear messages about what is involved.

Applying these principles usually produces response rates for voluntary questionnaire completion in excess of 70%. In some organisations over 90% of staff volunteer to take part in the audit. Our response rates would be considerably lower if the preparation and briefing were inadequate.

Reporting back to individual employees on their own personal pressure profile is a vital part of the process and should be heavily promoted as a reason why they should get involved in the audit process. Also of vital importance is feedback on the aggregated results, and demonstrating what the next steps are going to be.

Checklists for success

Checklist for a successful survey

- Don't start a survey or audit unless you intend to do something with the results.
- Be clear about your reasons for introducing an audit and be open about how you will share the results.
- Make sure that everyone in the organisation is aware that a survey is taking place and why particular groups have been selected to take part.
- Involve your staff in the audit process from the beginning.
- Make sure that the senior management team buys into and actively supports the stress audit. If they are unable to support the investigation they are unlikely to commit resources to the interventions.
- Make sure that your questionnaire is comprehensive and compact and measures what it's meant to measure.
- Keep people informed of progress at every stage.
- Be open and honest in your communication.
- Make sure that any interventions that arise from the survey are clearly linked to the survey so that staff can see that their voices have been heard.
- Identify and act on 'quick wins'.
- Don't over-analyse; if it's obvious that something needs to be done, then do it!
- Take care of the casualties. In any organisation a stress audit will bring hidden issues to the surface and, more importantly, provide an opportunity for people at risk to seek help. Make sure that professional help is readily and easily available.
- Involve as many people as possible in the audit; don't be too selective.
- Support the data with small group discussions to 'sense check' and explain the findings.
- Ensure that everyone involved in the audit process is aware of the findings and the recommendations.
- Set realistic goals; don't raise expectations that you can't meet.

- Develop small-scale sustainable interventions; don't waste resources on 'big bang' initiatives that will fade away.
- Don't turn those who are well into the worried well. Deliver the feedback in a positive and supportive manner.
- Work hard to maximise the response rates, carry out briefing sessions, involve management and, if present, unions in actively promoting participation.

There is, therefore, much more to a stress audit than sending out a lot of questionnaires!

For more information contact:
Dr Stephen Williams
Resource Systems
Claro Court
Claro Road
Harrogate
HG1 4BA
+ 44 (0) 1423 529 529
email: info@resourcesystems.co.uk
www.resourcesystems.co.uk

Lesley Cooper
WorkingWell Ltd
80 Fleet Street
London
EC4Y 1ET
+44 (0) 207 427 0020
email: info@workingwell.co.uk
www.workingwell.co.uk

BUSINESSHEALTH

Leading the way in private and public sector stress management

Businesshealth Group plc

T: 020 7004 2500

enquiries@BHGplc.com

F: 020 7004 2501

www.BHGplc.com

Glossary

Term	Description
Anxiety	A longer-term feeling of unease or discomfort
Contentment	Feeling generally satisfied about your state of mind
Control	The extent to which you *feel* able to influence and control events
Coping	The things that you do to deal with and manage problems
Drive	A strong desire to succeed and achieve results
Organisation culture and climate	The 'feel' or 'atmosphere' within your place of work
Peace of mind	Feeling settled, without major worries
Personality	The individual character of a person
Problem focus coping	Dealing with the cause of the problem
Recognition	The value that others place upon you
Relationships	How well you get on with the people around you, particularly those at work
Resilience	The ability to 'bounce back' from setbacks or problems
Self-esteem	The value that you place upon yourself
Support	The help you get by discussing problems or situations with other people
Type A behaviour	Rushed, competitive, urgent way of life
Wellbeing	Feeling good, both mentally and physically

Appendix

Almost anything can be a source of pressure and people perceive things differently. The following items are all potential sources of pressure. Please rate them according to the degree of pressure you perceive they have placed on you during the last three months. Please answer the questions as they actually apply to you. Do not answer theoretically. For example, if a question asks about pressure from managing your staff and you do not have anyone working for you, you should answer ①, i.e. no pressure. Do not answer on the basis of how much pressure you would expect to feel if you had to manage staff.

Sources of pressure in your job

	1 Very definitely is not a source	2 Definitely is not a source	3 Generally is not a source	4 Generally is a source	5 Definitely is a source		6 Very definitely is a source
1. Managing or supervising the work of other people.	1	2	3	4	5	6
2. Taking my work home.	1	2	3	4	5	6
3. Underpromotion – working at a level below my level of ability.	1	2	3	4	5	6
4. Inadequate guidance and back-up from superiors.	1	2	3	4	5	6
5. Lack of consultation and communication.	1	2	3	4	5	6
6. Not being able to 'switch off' at home.	1	2	3	4	5	6
7. Keeping up with new techniques, ideas, technology or innovations.	1	2	3	4	5	6
8. Inadequate or poor quality of training/management development.	1	2	3	4	5	6
9. Attending meetings.	1	2	3	4	5	6
10. Lack of social support by people at work.	1	2	3	4	5	6

Table A.1 *PMI questions – extract from sources of pressure section of the Pressure Management Indicator* Copyright © 2001 Resource Systems, Harrogate, UK. Used with permission.

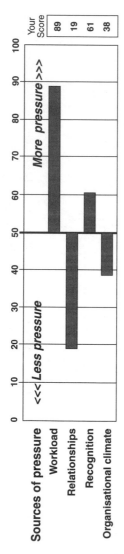

Sources of pressure

<<< *Less pressure*   *More pressure* >>>

	Your Score
Workload	89
Relationships	19
Recognition	61
Organisational climate	38

Workload: your results

You report much more pressure from your workload than the average person. Work overload obviously makes very heavy demands on you. You should consider whether this is because of the amount of work or the difficulty of the work you do. You should then take steps to reduce this source of pressure; for example, by talking to your manager about reducing the volume of work or by taking extra training to deal with the more challenging aspects of your job.

Relationships: your results

Your score shows that you do not feel under too much pressure from relationships with people at work. You feel comfortable with the people around you.

Recognition: your results

The chart shows that pressure from recognition, career progression or development is about the same for you as for other people. There may be some issues that concern you but they are not a major source of pressure to you.

Organisational climate: your results

Your results show that the climate of your organisation is a source of pressure for you but this is not excessive. On the whole, the demands placed on you by your working environment are about the same as for most other people.

Table A.2   *PMI personal profile – extract from sources of pressure section of the Pressure Management Indicator*
Copyright © 2001 Resource Systems, Harrogate, UK. Used with permission.

Index